**ROD CAREW, VIDA BLUE, AND BIG KLU**
Connie Mack, Stan Hack, and Max Flack
Herman Franks, Howard Shanks, and Ernie Banks
Wally Pipp, Ewell the Whip, and Leo the Lip

These are just a few of the famous and familiar names who have contributed to the lore and legend of baseball.

**But:** Who hit into the only all-Cuban triple play?
Who was the first player to wear a number?
What two players were called "Paw Paw"?
What pitcher holds the record for most stolen bases?
Who set a World Series record in one year and tied it the next?

This collection of tantalizing tidbits of baseball trivia will boggle the mind and joggle the memory of even the most devoted fan.
**Baseball aficionados will find it IRRESISTIBLE.**

"A sure winner in any game of one-upmanship."
**RED SMITH**

"Everything you've always wanted to know about baseball but were afraid to look up. . . ."

**DAVE ANDERSON**
The New York Times

"The type of information that makes for an 'instant expert.'"
**CLIFF KACHLINE**, HISTORIAN
Baseball Hall of Fame

"All the facts and figures that make baseball the enduring sport it is."

**SEYMOUR SIWOFF**
Elias Sports Bureau

# The BASEBALL TRIVIA Book

## BY BERT RANDOLPH SUGAR

Original Title: *Who Was Harry Steinfeldt?*
*and Other Baseball Trivia Questions*

**PLAYBOY PAPERBACKS**

THE BASEBALL TRIVIA BOOK

Copyright © 1976, 1982 by Bert Randolph Sugar

Cover photograph copyright © 1981 by PEI Books, Inc.

Published simultaneously in the United States and Canada by Playboy Paperbacks, New York, New York. Printed in the United States of America. Library of Congress Catalog Card Number: 75-44566. Revised edition.

Books are available at quantity discounts for promotional and industrial use. For further information, write to Premium Sales, Playboy Paperbacks, 1633 Broadway, New York, New York 10019.

ISBN: 0-872-16824-7

First printing June 1976.
Fifth printing May 1982.

# TABLE OF CONTENTS

# FOREWORD

*A civilization defines itself by its trivia.*
ARTHUR M. SCHLESINGER, SR.

Trivia was invented on July 5, 1839, in Cooperstown, New York, by Abner Doubleday's mother. One night at the dinner table, she asked the question "Who invented baseball?"

Her son Abner said, "What's baseball?"

No one knew the answer. Because Abner so loved his mother (she baked terrific apple pies), he became obsessed with finding the answer to her question. Doubleday spent most of his youth searching for the answer. Finally, as a young man, the tortured and frustrated Doubleday hit upon an idea. To satisfy his mother's curiosity, *he* would invent baseball (since it seemed no one else had). The day after he invented it, a delighted Doubleday came to his mother with the answer.

She said, "Well, I'm glad to know, but after all these years the answer has become trivial."

Historians may quibble about details, but that is essentially how two sports were invented simultaneously by one family. The popularity of baseball trivia led imitators to invent football and basketball trivia and people to ask trivia questions about movies, radio and TV. America owes the Doubledays plenty. They didn't even get merchandising rights.

Baseball trivia is important. It helps people earn money and make friends. At a bar someone will say, "Betcha five bucks ya can't name the starting lineup of the 1948 St. Louis Browns." Knowing trivia is like knowing magic tricks or how to play the piano. You can thrill and amaze people at parties.

Playing baseball trivia gives sportswriters something to do while waiting for the relief pitcher to come into the game. It also gives relief pitchers something to do when they're *not* coming into the game. I've spent hours (too many) in bullpens across the country asking and answering trivia questions like: What regular first baseman got a headache, giving Lou Gehrig a chance to play? Answer: Wally Pipp. Question number two: When did Wally Pipp recover from his headache? Answer: Never. Once Gehrig started playing, Pipp *always* had a headache. My favorites were insiders' trivia, like: Which hand did Ralph Houk use to punch Ryne Duren during the argument on an airplane in 1960? Answer: His left (although Houk was ambidextrous when it came to punching).

One of my greatest thrills in life is to be the *answer* to several trivia questions: Who was the winning pitcher in the last two World Series games won by the Yankees? What player holds the World Series record (37 times) for losing his hat? And who was the first Yankee pitcher to be driven in from the bullpen rather than walk in? The answer, as you might know by now, is:

JIM BOUTON

Englewood, New Jersey

P.S. One final trivia question: Who is Arthur M. Schlesinger, Sr., and what was his batting average?

# PREFACE

If you grew up in Washington, D.C., during the late Forties and early Fifties, you were reduced to finding nourishment in every scrap of information about baseball and memorizing its history. For the baseball team itself was less than exciting, proving right with every passing year the wags who had coined the phrase "Washington: First in war, first in peace and last in the American League" some 40 years earlier.

As you jumped aboard the trolley after cutting classes, or more accurately hung onto the back of it for a free ride down to Seventh and Georgia Avenue, you somehow looked forward as much to seeing some of your old friends with whom you could share past historical highlights as you did to watching the sorry athletes who called themselves Washington Senators cavort around Griffith Stadium. Sure, we had our Mickey Vernons and Stan Spences and Early Wynns, and even later our Herbie Plews and our Sam Dentes and our Wayne Terwilligers, but that hardly seemed fair when the other teams had better-known players—even to us—and won more games. So we were reduced to living vicariously and spouting our baseball facts to keep up both our interest in the game at hand and our faith in baseball.

From that very first day when I got a job selling the bulldog edition of the *Washington Post* at night games in Griffith Stadium and wandered through the gates free as a courtesy from the gatekeeper to the *Post*, down through the years when I would go to the corner at Seventh and Georgia to buy three nickel papers, tuck them under my arm and wave at the gatekeeper, who still thought I was selling papers, not just gate-crashing, I was hooked on baseball. (And, anyway, gate-crashing into a Redskins game was tougher. They had some funny rule that any child small enough to sit on his parent's lap could get in free if he could walk under the turnstile. And for years I duck-walked into the park under the disbelieving eyes of the ticket-takers who were certain I was past puberty and that the person with me wasn't my parent. All that duck-walking gave my legs cramps, and I decided I'd rather buy just three papers and wave my way past the gatekeeper 77 times a year than stoop over and duck-walk my way past a ticket-taker six times a year.)

I lived, ate and slept baseball and baseball facts. If I had a thought, it was about and for the Senators. I even took to calling the owner, Clark Griffith, on the phone to give him, free of charge, any and all advice I could think of. I would call him any hour, since he made himself accessible back in those days of six-digit dialing by listing his number in the phone book for any wide-eyed baseball fan to see. Accessible, that is, except for the hours of 7:00 to 7:30 on Mondays, Wednesdays and Fridays, when his wife informed me that no one could interrupt Mr. Griffith in the middle of his favorite radio show, "The Lone Ranger."

But as you grew up, your world grew with you. And the facts, which used to be only about the Senators, now became generic. My friends, whom I used to call childlike names, like "Fats" and "Stinky," also bombarded me with Yankee facts (ugh!) or National League facts (who were they?) or, heaven forbid, minor-league facts, often in the form of questions that called for an answer. This was the beginning of a new sport, a sport which was to become known to us as "trivia."

Just as there were those of us who used to stand outside Griffith Stadium seeking companionship and questions, so were there those who were hanging around Addison Avenue, Jerome Avenue, Commonwealth Avenue or Montague Street or any of the other streets and avenues that bordered a ball park, hungry for more than just the game that was about to be played or had just been played that afternoon. This was our life. We cherished the questions and, even more, relished giving the correct answers. First, for the compliments grudgingly paid for the correct answer to a hard "trivia" question, and then for the money even more grudgingly given for the correct answer to another more difficult question. It was a slow week if I didn't win a few bucks then, and an even slower week later when "trivia" couldn't pay for all my bar bills at law school.

For baseball is a figure-oriented world, as no other pastime is or could be. From that first day when I learned the rudiments of double-entry bookkeeping by figuring out that the box score of one team, with all its at-bats and outs, had to tally exactly against that of the other team, down through the years when I began to "collect" the hundreds of thousands of significant and insignificant statistics that baseball continually generated, it has been my first love. And these details, these numbers, have forged a bond between baseball fans the world over who thirst to read box scores and record books and batting averages as no football, basketball or hockey fan ever could. It's the endless stream of statistics and the lore and legend of the game that unite baseball fans—regardless of their backgrounds, whether they be factory workers or executives, students or professors, bartenders or patrons—into collectors of trivia, or "triviots."

I was fortunate indeed to find a body of "triviots" out there who were instrumental in helping me develop some of the great "you can't look 'em up" trivia questions found in these pages. I'm indebted enough to them to thank each one of them personally here and now. Thank you, Cliff Kachline of the Baseball Hall of Fame, and Bob Davids of the Society of American Baseball Research, and Art Berke of the baseball commissioner's office, Larry Bortstein, and Dave Neft, and Red Smith, and Eddie Gold, and

Dick Costello and his electric Xerox machine, and Bill Himmelman, and Walter Gibson and Barry Landers of the Yankees, and Paul Lapolla and Ed Kuhn of Playboy, and Larry Fritsch, and Ben Weiser, and Keith Olberman, and Marty Appel, and Jim Bouton, and all the others who helped me, both known and unknown to me, down through the years in framing these fun questions.

As for the ultimate question, asked by the one I thank most of all, my wife: "Who's interested in all that baseball trivia?" We are—we all are!

# 1ST INNING

## THE PLAYERS

*Who was the third baseman in the Tinker-Evers-Chance infield?*

Harry Steinfeldt was denied immortality when his name couldn't be worked into Franklin P. Adams's immortal quatrain, "Baseball's Sad Lexicon," along with the names Tinker, Evers and Chance. And so he remained another of baseball's "Who's he?"s despite the fact that he played in the major leagues for 14 years and alongside Tinker, Evers and Chance from 1906 to 1910 on four pennant-winning teams.

Adams's verse, first published in the *New York Globe* in 1908 after the Cubs had beaten the Giants in the famous "Merkle Muff" game, gained instant immortality for the three Cub infielders with these famous words:

> These are the saddest of possible words,
>     Tinker-to-Evers-to-Chance.
> Trio of Bear Cubs fleeter than birds,
>     Tinker-to-Evers-to-Chance.
> Ruthlessly pricking our gonfalon bubble,
> Making a Giant hit into a double,
> Words that are weighty with nothing but trouble.
> Tinker-to-Evers-to-Chance.

It would have been a more proper question to ask "What is a 'gonfalon'?" (which means standard or, in this case, flag) than to ask who Harry Steinfeldt was. For Harry Steinfeldt led the Cubs to victory in the 1907 World Series with a .471 batting average, a World Series high not only for that Series but the third highest mark ever for a five-game Series. And Steinfeldt produced during the regular season play as well, leading the National League in RBI's with 83 in 1906, to lead the Cubs into another Series, hitting .327, second best in the League. All in all, Harry Steinfeldt's credentials are impressive—14 years of play and a lifetime average of .267 in the era of the dead ball.

But either because the Cubs beat out New York's finest,

the Giants, for five straight years—including the hotly contested 1908 pennant race, which was decided when Evers spotted Merkle's failure to touch second—or because Joe Tinker completely mastered New York's ace right-hander, Christy Mathewson, or because Frank Chance was then, in name and in action, "The Peerless Leader," or merely because Steinfeldt's name wouldn't fit into the rhyme, Harry Steinfeldt, the third baseman for those same Chicago Cubs, became merely another "Who's he?"

*Who was the only man to lead his league in earned-run average and not pitch a shutout?*

New York Giants' pitcher Dave Koslo started 38 games in 1949, winning 11 and losing 14. He led the National League in fewest walks per nine-inning game, fewest hits per nine innings and ERA, with 2.50. But Koslo did not pitch a shutout in accomplishing this feat. His lifetime record shows 92 wins and 107 losses, with 16 shutouts, but none came in 1949, the year he was the only pitcher ever to lead his league in ERA without pitching a single shutout.

*Who appeared as a pinch hitter, in his last major-league appearance, in the game in which Babe Ruth hit his 60th home run?*

Although most of the 10,000 fans at Yankee Stadium that afternoon of September 30, 1927, came to see history being made and thought they had when Babe Ruth hit his 60th home run off Washington's Tom Zachary in the bottom of the eighth, history of another sort was made the next inning. Washington opened the top of the ninth by sending up a pinch hitter for Zachary. The pinch hitter was the former great Washington pitching ace, Walter Johnson, who was making his last major-league appearance. It was not unusual for the Senators to employ "The Big Train" as a pinch hitter. During his 21 years with

Washington, Johnson had been to bat 110 times as a pinch hitter and had amassed a batting mark of .348 during 1927, with two home runs among his 16 hits. Just two years before, Johnson had hit .433 during the season and had amassed 549 hits during his career, making him one of only four men—together with Joe Wood, Red Ruffing and Happy Jack Stivetts—to have over 100 wins and 500 hits.

### *Who hit into the only all-Cuban triple play?*

Dorrel Norman Elvert "Whitey" Herzog, outfielder for the Kansas City A's in 1960, hit into the only all-Cuban triple play against the Washington Senators. With Camilio Pascual pitching for the old Senators in their last year of existence before moving to Minnesota, Herzog hit a line drive which was turned into a Pascual-to-Julio Becquer-to-Jose Valdivielso triple play, the only time a triple play in America's National Pastime was ever executed by three Cubans.

### *What two players were traded for themselves?*

Although one of baseball's most time-honored axioms is "The best trades are the ones that aren't made," some of those that have been made are beauts. Managers have been traded for each other, coaches for each other and even two players have been traded for themselves. Two journeymen ballplayers—Harry Chiti and Clint Courtney —were both constantly being shuttled back and forth to teams looking for help. Courtney played with seven different clubs during his 11 years in the big league, and Chiti with four in 10 years. But twice these two players were traded for themselves. It happened this way: Many trades are consummated because a team needs immediate help in a particular position and doesn't have a player needed by the other team in the deal; therefore, they take the player with the rather vague promise that they will send "a player to be named later." In two cases that "player to be named later" was the player originally sent over to initiate the trade—Harry Chiti and Clint Courtney —so each trade read "Harry Chiti traded for Harry Chiti," and "Clint Courtney traded for Clint Courtney."

The minor leagues have also had their unusual trades. Pitcher Joe Martina was once acquired by the New Orleans Pelicans of the Southern Association for a sack of oysters. And first baseman Jack Fenton was acquired by San Francisco of the Pacific Coast League for a carton of prunes. But perhaps the most classic of all trades was the one engineered by Joe Engel, "The Barnum of the Bushes," who was president of the Chattanooga Lookouts of the Southern Association from 1929 through the Sixties. Engel once traded shortstop Johnny Jones to Charlotte in the Sally League for a 25-pound turkey, and then invited some 25 sportswriters to taste the "new meat" on the team at a turkey dinner. Afterward Engel claimed, "I think I got the worst of that deal. That was a mighty tough turkey."

*What candidate received the most votes ever in a Hall of Fame ballot?*

Sandy Koufax, almost unanimously elected to the Hall of Fame at the youngest age of any candidate by the members of the Baseball Writers Association, also received the most votes ever received, 344, in the 1972 balloting.

*Name the man for whom Eddie Gaedel pinch-hit.*

On July 19, 1951, baseball's most improbable batter opened the second game of a doubleheader between the eighth-place St. Louis Browns and the fifth-place Detroit Tigers. The batter's name was Eddie Gaedel, a 3'7" midget who wore the number ⅛ on the back of his uniform and carried a Little League bat to the plate. Up to a few minutes before, Gaedel had been part of the Falstaff beer party, coming out of a cake to help the Browns' sponsor celebrate its birthday. But now Gaedel, the product of Bill Veeck's fertile imagination, was moving into the batter's box to pinch-hit for the Browns' scheduled lead-off batter, Frank Saucier. Saucier, who was to play just 18 games in the majors and come to bat just 14 times with one hit, gained more immortality by having Gaedel pinch-hit for him—and get on base to open the game—than he did by his own big-league exploits.

*Who were the only two ballplayers traded between games of a doubleheader by the two opposing teams, playing the first game for their old teams and the second game for their new teams?*

Just as Bill Veeck had once considered trading Norm Cash from the White Sox to the Yankees for Andy Carey so that the headlines could read "Cash and Carey," one of the strangest trades was one that sent two players on teams that were opposing each other in a doubleheader to their new teams between games so they could suit up for the second game and play against one another again—in new uniforms. Between games of a morning-afternoon doubleheader on May 30, 1922, outfielder Cliff Heathcote of the Chicago Cubs was traded to the St. Louis Cardinals for outfielder Max Flack of the Cards. Both went out on the field in the second game for their new teams, this time Flack for the Cubs and Heathcote for the Cards, and even though both had hit safely in the morning game, both went hitless in the nightcap for their new teams.

*Who was the first player to wear a number?*

When Cleveland Indian left fielder Jack Graney led off the first inning on June 26, 1916, he became the first modern major-league player to come to bat wearing a number. The number, attached to the player's sleeve, was used as an identifying mark, as were the numbers affixed to the backs of the St. Louis Browns players in 1923. But the players, rebelling at the ridicule heaped on them by the fans, who called them "convicts," asked to have them taken off. The numbers came off, not to reappear on players' backs until the Yankees wore them—and retained them—in 1929.

Jack Graney also was the first player to face Babe Ruth when the young left-hander came up to the Red Sox in 1914 from Providence, and further secured his niche in the Baseball Trivia Hall of Fame by being the first former ballplayer to become a broadcaster, broadcasting Indian games for over 20 years.

*What player was in uniform on the day Roger Maris hit his 61st home run in New York and Hank Aaron hit his 715th home run in Atlanta?*

The one player who was in uniform for two of base-ball's most momentous moments was pitcher Al Downing, a member of the New York Yankees in 1961 when Roger Maris hit his 61st home run off Tracy Stallard of the Red Sox and the pitcher who delivered the home-run pitch that Hank Aaron hit into the left-field bullpen for his 715th home run. Downing, who came up to the Yankees in 1961 and posted an 0–1 record at the end of the season, went back down to the minors for most of the 1962 season and part of 1963. He then won 65 games over the next six years for the Yankees before being sent down to the minors again. Traded to Oakland in December of 1969, he spent part of the next season with the A's before being traded again to Milwaukee. At the beginning of the 1971 season he was sent to the Los Angeles Dodgers, where he found his form, turned in his only 20-game season and was elected "Comeback Player of the Year." Three years later and some 14 years after he had seen

Maris break one of Ruth's cherished records, Al Downing took the mound on April 8, 1974, for the Los Angeles Dodgers and personally witnessed Hank Aaron break another, as Aaron, wearing number 44 for the Braves, hit a pitch from number 44 of the Dodgers that didn't quite stay outside Aaron's strike area.

*What player appeared in 150 games the most consecutive years?*

Although Lou Gehrig appeared in 2130 consecutive games over 13 complete seasons, he only appeared in 149 in 1935, the total number the Yankees played that year. The major-league record for the most consecutive years of 150 or more games is 13, held by Willie Mays, from 1954 through 1966. The American League record is 11 and is held by Nellie Fox, from 1952 through 1962.

*Name the one player who was in uniform at four of the last five games in which a player hit four home runs.*

Only one active, eligible player—pitcher Billy Loes—was at four of the last five games in which four homers were hit. Loes's career spans just 11 years with three clubs—the Brooklyn Dodgers, the Baltimore Orioles and the San Francisco Giants—and by some strange quirk of fate he was on hand and in uniform when Gil Hodges hit four in Brooklyn's Ebbets Field on August 31, 1950; when Milwaukee's Joe Adcock hit four also in Ebbets Field on July 31, 1954; when Cleveland's Rocky Colavito hit four at Baltimore's Memorial Stadium on June 10, 1959; and when San Francisco's Willie Mays hit four at Milwaukee's County Stadium on April 30, 1961. Loes, although in uniform for all four, only appeared in one of those four games, winning the game in which Mays hit his four.

*Who was the only Yankee on hand both on the day Lou Gehrig started his consecutive-game streak and when he ended it?*

Wally Pipp, the first baseman for the Yankees, complained of a headache on June 1, 1925, and took the day off. Manager Miller Huggins inserted a rawboned Columbia graduate named Lou Gehrig and Pipp never got his position back, finally being traded at the end of the season to Cincinnati. Some 14 years later, Pipp, then a salesman in his hometown of Grand Rapids, Michigan, was making a business trip to Detroit and decided to take in a ball game. The Tigers were playing the Yankees and on the day that Pipp attended the game, May 2, 1939, he saw his replacement, Lou Gehrig, voluntarily take himself out of the ball game after 2130 consecutive games, including 885 consecutively at the position Pipp had relinquished to him—first base. Pipp was one of the 11,379 fans who showed up at Detroit's Briggs Stadium that afternoon to see Gehrig's replacement, Babe Dahlgren, get two hits and drive in two runs as the Yankees walloped the Tigers 22–2.

*Who became the regular Yankee catcher the day Lou Gehrig replaced Wally Pipp at first base?*

June 1, 1925, was notable because Lou Gehrig started his 2130-consecutive-game streak. But it was also noteworthy to Benny Bengough, because on that day the little catcher was moved into the Yankee starting lineup, too, replacing Wally Schang.

*Who was the youngest player to appear in an American League game?*

When Carl Scheib took the mound for the Philadelphia A's on September 6, 1943, he was but 16 years, 8 months and 5 days old, the youngest player ever to appear in an

American League game, but older than Joe Nuxhall, the youngest ever, who appeared as a pitcher for the Reds at the age of 15 years, 10 months and 11 days. However, the youngest player in the history of organized ball was a 12-year-old youth who was the batboy for the Fitzgerald team in the Georgia State League. With the score 13–0 against the hometown Fitzgerald team and the crowd chanting "Put in the batboy," manager Charles Ridgeway of Fitzgerald consulted the home-plate umpire and then sent in the batboy, Charles Relford, as a pinch hitter. Relford, who was black and broke the color barrier in the Georgia State League, grounded sharply to third. In the top of the ninth he went to center field, where he handled one ball cleanly and made a sensational catch of a sinking line drive.

The league directors met the next day and fired the umpire and fined and suspended the manager for the incident. Owner Ace Adams, former pitcher for the New York Giants, took over as interim manager and also dropped the batboy. But young Relford had made history, as the youngest player ever in the history of organized baseball, eclipsing the youthful appearance of the then youngest player ever to appear in an organized ball game, Joe Schultz, who, in 1931 at the age of 13 had pinch-hit for the Houston team his father owned (and was to later become a coach with the St. Louis Cardinals and manager of the Seattle Pilots), and also eclipsing the records of Scheib and Nuxhall.

*What player wore the name of his hometown on the back of his uniform?*

Bill Voiselle, who pitched for the New York Giants, Boston Braves and Chicago Cubs from 1942 through 1950, was the pride and joy of Ninety-Six, South Carolina (population 1345 in Greenwood County). So it was only right and proper that he was assigned a uniform with the number 96 on the back of it. Coming up in 1942, Voiselle blossomed into a 21-game winner in 1944. The next season number 96 started where he left off, winning six straight at one point in the season. But then in his next start against the defending champion St. Louis Cardinals he grooved an 0-2 pitch to the ever-dangerous Johnny Hopp, and Hopp tripled to beat Voiselle and the Giants. Manager Mel Ott fined Voiselle $500 for throwing a strike with an 0-2 count. Ott later rescinded the fine, but Voiselle took it hard and never was the same again. He soon gravitated out of baseball for good, taking number 96 out of baseball with him, never to be seen again in the majors.

### Which two players were called "Paw Paw"?

Many players have borne the names of their hometowns as part of their names. Sam Crawford was known as "Wahoo" Sam because he came from Wahoo, Nebraska; Bill James of the Miracle 1914 Braves was called "Seattle" Bill, not only because he came from Seattle but to distinguish him from "Big" Bill James, who pitched in the American League at the same time; and Clint Hartung was known as the "Hondo Hurricane" partly because he came from Hondo, Texas, and partly because of his press notices, which he failed to live up to.

But the little town of Paw Paw, Michigan, in the southwest part of the state, some 20 miles from Kalamazoo, population 2970, has claimed two major-leaguers. The two players nicknamed "Paw Paw" were "Paw Paw" Bill Killefer, who caught the great Grover Cleveland Alexander for 11 years for both the Phillies and the Cubs, and "Paw Paw" Charlie Maxwell, who played for the Tigers in the Fifties and always seemed able to deliver a Sunday home run in front of the Tiger fans. Killefer, from Bloomingdale, Michigan, had attended school in Paw Paw, ten miles from his home, and Maxwell originally hailed from Lawton, Michigan, just a few miles down the road from the thriving metropolis of Paw Paw and only half as large.

Thus, the little town of Paw Paw has insinuated its name into the National Pastime more than towns 100 times as large because of two of her favorite (and adopted) sons.

*What modern player scored in the most consecutive games?*

Although Billy Hamilton scored in 23 straight games before the turn of the century, Ted Kluszewski holds the modern record for scoring in the most consecutive games, by scoring at least one run in 17 consecutive games, from August 27 to September 13, 1954. He also holds some sort of honor for being the first player to have his name spelled wrong on the back of his jersey (while a member of the White Sox in 1960).

*What two Fordham University second basemen both later became Cardinals?*

Second baseman–shortstop Frankie Frisch, graduated directly from the Fordham campus in 1919 to stardom with the New York Giants, breaking in as a pinch hitter for Hal Chase, later becoming the playing manager of the St. Louis Cardinals. Nine years earlier Frankie Spellman, later to become Francis Cardinal Spellman of the New York archdiocese, was the second-string second baseman for Fordham, behind Jack Coffey, who played for the Braves and the Red Sox and became Fordham's athletic director.

Just as the current bar favorite, "What six American vice-presidents are not buried in the United States?" presupposes they're dead (and they're not, the answer being Nixon, Humphrey, Agnew, Ford, Rockefeller and Mondale), this question presupposes that both became St. Louis Cardinals. They didn't.

*Who was the only man to be actively playing in Babe Ruth's last year and in Hank Aaron's first year?*

Phil Cavarretta, who came up as an 18-year-old first baseman for the Cubs in 1934 and played through 1955, the last two years as a member of the crosstown White Sox, is the only player to span the years between 1935 (Ruth's last) and 1954 (Aaron's first).

*What player played in the most major-league games before he turned 20? What player had the most home runs before he turned 20?*

Robin Yount, Milwaukee's young shortstop, of whom one sportscaster said during a night game, "I wonder if he has to call home to see if he can stay out late," set the record for the most games played as a teen-ager in 1975, surpassing Mel Ott's total two days before his 20th birthday on September 16, 1975. Yount also came to bat more than any other teen-ager in the majors, eclipsing Phil Cavarretta's old mark. The "teeny-bopper" who hit more home runs than any other teen-ager was Tony Conigliaro. "Tony C." hit 24 of his 164 lifetime homers before he turned 20 on January 7, 1965, to lead all teen-age players in circuit clouts. Other notable teen-agers who achieved some statistics and stardom by the time they turned 20 include Ty Cobb, Al Kaline and Rusty Staub. Their teen-age records are shown below:

## TEEN-AGE RECORDS

| Teen-ager | Years | G | AB | R | H | 2B | 3B | HR | RBI | SB | Bat. |
|---|---|---|---|---|---|---|---|---|---|---|---|
| Melvin Ott | 1926–28 | 241 | 658 | 99 | 209 | 35 | 7 | 19 | 100 | 6 | .318* |
| P. Cavarretta | 1934–36 | 221 | 856 | 120* | 234* | 36 | 14* | 14 | 117* | 8 | .274 |
| Ed Kranepool | 1962–64 | 208 | 699 | 69 | 166 | 32 | 6 | 12 | 59 | 4 | .237 |
| Al Kaline | 1953–54 | 168 | 532 | 51 | 146 | 18 | 3 | 5 | 45 | 10 | .274 |
| Cass Michaels | 1943–45 | 158 | 520 | 51 | 121 | 12 | 6 | 2 | 59 | 8 | .233 |
| Fred Lindstrom | 1924–25 | 156 | 435 | 62 | 122 | 18 | 13 | 4 | 37 | 8 | .280 |
| Rusty Staub | 1963 | 150 | 513 | 43 | 115 | 17 | 4 | 6 | 45 | 0 | .224 |
| Ty Cobb | 1905–06 | 140 | 508 | 64 | 149 | 21 | 5 | 2 | 49 | 24* | .293 |
| T. Conigliaro | 1964 | 111 | 404 | 69 | 117 | 21 | 2 | 24* | 52 | 2 | .290 |
| Robin Yount | 1974–75 | 243* | 857* | 109 | 223 | 41* | 6 | 11 | 75 | 18 | .260 |

* Teen-age leader

*Who was the last man to steal second, third and home in a single inning?*

Dave Nelson of the Texas Rangers stole second, third and home against the Cleveland Indians on August 30, 1974, the last man to accomplish the base-stealing "hat trick" and the first since Rod Carew did it in 1969. In fact Nelson, Carew and Don Kolloway of the Chicago White Sox, who did it back in 1941, are the only three to steal their way around the bases in the last 46 years. Ty Cobb holds the record with three steals around the bases, followed by Honus Wagner, Jack Tavener and Max Carey with two. The only pitcher to steal second, third and home in an inning was Red Faber of the White Sox, whose feat is somewhat tarnished because he tried to get thrown out to speed up a rain-threatened game, but the A's, trying to delay the game, made only a token half-hearted effort to catch him. Ten men in the National League and 20 in the American have pulled off this base-stealing sweep:

### BASE-STEALING SWEEPS

| | | | | |
|---|---|---|---|---|
| **NL** Honus Wagner, Pitt. | Sept. 25 1907 | **AL** Ty Cobb, Detroit | July | 4 1912 |
| Hans Lobert, Cin. | Sept. 27 1908 | Joe Jackson, Clev. | Aug. | 11 1912 |
| Honus Wagner, Pitt. | May 2 1909 | Eddie Collins, Phil. | Sept. | 22 1912 |
| Dode Paskert, Cin. | May 23 1910 | Ed Ainsmith, Wash. | June | 26 1913 |
| Wilbur Good, Chi. | Aug. 18 1915 | Fred Maisel, N.Y. | Aug. | 17 1915 |
| Jim Johnstone, Bkn. | Sept. 22 1916 | Red Faber* Chi. | July | 14 1915 |
| Greasy Neale, Cin. | Aug. 15 1919 | Dan Moeller, Wash. | July | 19 1915 |
| Max Carey, Pitt. | Aug. 13 1923 | Buck Weaver, Chi. | Sept. | 6 1919 |
| Max Carey, Pitt. | May 26 1925 | Bobby Roth, Wash. | May | 31 1920 |
| H. Hendrick, Bkn. | June 12 1928 | Bob Meusel, N.Y. | May | 16 1927 |
| **AL** Dave Fultz, Phil. | Sept. 4 1902 | Jack Tavener, Det. | July | 10 1927 |
| Bill Donovan, Det. | May 7 1906 | Jack Tavener, Det. | July | 25 1928 |
| Bill Coughlin, Det. | June 4 1906 | Don Kolloway, Chi. | June | 28 1941 |
| Ty Cobb, Detroit | July 22 1909 | Rod Carew, Minn. | May | 18 1969 |
| Ty Cobb, Detroit | July 12 1911 | Dave Nelson, Texas | Aug. | 30 1974 |

*When Ron Hunt was hit by pitches 50 times in 1971 to set the all-time record, who was the runner-up in the category?*

In 1971, when Ron Hunt of the Montreal Expos was hit by pitches a record 50 times, the runner-up was teammate Rusty Staub with but nine. Hunt broke the all-time record previously held by Hughie Jennings of the old Baltimore Orioles, who was reportedly hit by pitches 49 times in 1896. In so running away with the category, Hunt also established an all-time five-to-one lead over his nearest competitor, the most total domination of any batting category, as shown below:

### BATTING DEPARTMENT RECORD RUNAWAYS

| Year | League | Dept. | Leader | | Runner-up | |
|------|--------|-------|--------|---|-----------|---|
| 1971 | NL | HBP | Ron Hunt | 50 | Rusty Staub | 9 |
| 1962 | NL | SB | Maury Wills | 104 | Willie Davis | 32 |
| 1920 | AL | HR | Babe Ruth | 54 | Geo. Sisler | 19 |
| 1946 | NL | 3B | Stan Musial | 20 | Reese-Cavvy | 10 |
| 1904 | NL | 2B | Hans Wagner | 44 | Bus Mertes | 28 |
| 1946 | NL | Hits | Stan Musial | 228 | Dixie Walker | 184 |
| 1921 | AL | Runs | Babe Ruth | 177 | John Tobin | 132 |
| 1935 | AL | RBI | Hank Greenberg | 170 | Lou Gehrig | 119 |
| 1922 | NL | TB | Rogers Hornsby | 450 | Emil Meusel | 314 |
| 1901 | AL | Batting | Nap Lajoie | .426 | Mike Donlin | .340 |
| 1921 | AL | Slugging Average | Babe Ruth | .846 | Harry Heilmann | .606 |

*What player had the longest career in the majors playing under only one manager?*

Don Drysdale played his entire career under one manager, Walter Alston. Pitching for 14 years (1956–69) with the Brooklyn Dodgers and Los Angeles Dodgers, he thus had the longest career with *only one* manager. Other players like Eddie Plank and Christy Mathewson played for Connie Mack and John McGraw for 14 and 15 years, respectively, but ended their careers under other managers—in Mathewson's case the manager was himself. And while Drysdale holds the record for the longest career played under only one manager, Deacon Jim McGuire also holds a record of sorts, playing under 23 different managers during his 26-year career.

*Who played right field for the Yankees the year before Babe Ruth joined the team?*

Everyone knows that George Selkirk succeeded Babe Ruth in right field, but one of the men who preceded Ruth is known only to sports fans from his other life. For the right fielder in 1919, along with Sammy Vick, before the Yankees purchased Ruth from the Red Sox for $125,000 on January 3, 1920, was a young, 24-year-old outfielder from Chicago named George Stanley Halas. Yes, *that* George Halas. Halas played in 12 games for the 1919 Yankees, batting a mere .091, but was expected to contribute to the Yankees' 1920 pennant drive. However, Halas suffered a broken leg before the season began and went home to work as athletic director for the Staley Starch Company in nearby Decatur, Illinois. There he persuaded Staley to sponsor a team that would enter the newly formed National Football League. Halas rounded up several semi-pro athletes in the area, including a boy from Decatur named Chuck Dressen who would be the new team's quarterback, and a T-formation quarterback at that—football's first—and pursue a major-league career himself, both as a player and as a manager.

*Name the only four major-league baseball players who later served in Congress.*

Four former major-league baseball players have been elected to Congress—one to the Senate and three to the U.S. House of Representatives: Fred Brown, Wilmer Mizell, Pius Schwert and John Tener. The major-league player to have the most successful political career was Fred H. Brown, who played for the Boston Braves in 1901 and 1902. He served as governor of New Hampshire from 1923 through 1924, as U.S. senator from 1933 until 1939, and was nominated for the presidency at the 1924 Democratic Convention.

Wilmer "Vinegar Bend" Mizell, the former pitcher for

the St. Louis Cardinals and Pittsburgh Pirates for nine years, came from a little hamlet in Alabama that had a population of 37. According to Mizell, "When they had a telephone booth installed, they had to move the city limits out a few feet." Mizell served in the House of Representatives from 1969 through 1975 and is now the assistant secretary of commerce.

Pius Schwert appeared in just 11 games for the 1914 and 1915 Yankees as a catcher and from 1939 to 1941 was the elected representative of the same upstate New York district now represented by former football player Jackie Kemp.

John Tener was born in Tyrone County, Ireland, and found fame as a baseball player for Baltimore, Chicago and Pittsburgh before the turn of the century. After retiring he was elected to the House from 1909 through 1911, served as governor of the state of Pennsylvania from 1911 through 1915, and concurrently became president of the National League from 1913 until he resigned in 1918.

There might well have been a fifth ex-ballplayer in Congress if the voters in New Hampshire had known that one of the candidates running in a congressional primary was Jeff Tesreau. But Tesreau, the old Giant pitcher, was forced to use his Christian name, Charles, and the voters neither recognized nor elected him.

*Who was the only player born in Alaska?*

The only player to come from Alaska was Tom Sullivan, who caught one game for the 1925 Cincinnati Reds. Every other state in the union has been represented in the majors, including Hawaii by Mike Lum, and there have been players from 30 foreign countries. But only Tom Sullivan, born in Nome, has represented the 49th state.

*What player was active for the most years in organized baseball?*

The player active for the most years was Hall of Famer James "Orator" O'Rourke, who started his career with Mansfield in the National Association in 1872 and switched to Boston the next year. He played through 1893 in the majors, when he closed out his major-league career with Washington. From 1896 to 1907 he was the playing manager of Bridgeport in the Connecticut League. But for one game, the pennant-clinching game of the 1904 season, he caught for the New York Giants where at 52 he was the oldest player ever to play a full game in the majors, singling and scoring the deciding run.

For longevity, however, the record-holder is Nick Altrock, the old Chicago White Sox pitcher, who played his first game in 1898 for Louisville and would occasionally come off the coaching line long after his active days were over to pinch-hit and pinch-run for the Washington Senators. Altrock's last pinch-hitting effort was for the pennant-winning 1933 Senators, when he pinch-hit at the age of 56, 35 years after he had first appeared in a game for Louisville. Another long-timer was pitcher Tom "Lefty" George, who pitched from 1909 to 1944 but was active "only" 29 of those years, including parts of four years in the majors in which his record was an unimpressive 7-21.

*Who was the first major-league ballplayer to come to bat in a night game?*

Lou Chiozza was one of actress Tallulah Bankhead's favorites—not only because he played second for the New York Giants, but because, as Tallulah said, "He was born in Tallulah, Louisiana." But before Chiozza became a Giant, he played for the Philadelphia Phillies. And on May 24, 1935, after President Franklin D. Roosevelt switched on the lights in Cincinnati's Redland Field, Chiozza became the first man to come to bat in a

night baseball game, meekly going out on one of Paul
Derringer's fast balls.

The first home run ever hit in night baseball was hit
by Floyd "Babe" Herman, the Cincinnati outfielder, on
July 10, 1935, and the first no-hitter ever thrown at night
was Cincinnati's Johnny Vander Meer's second consecutive no-hitter in the inaugural of night baseball at Brooklyn's Ebbets Field on June 15, 1938.

> *Name the three catchers who played with New York
> teams during World War II all of whom had brothers
> who were also catchers.*

The three New York area teams during World War II
all had catchers who were part of a tandem act: They had
brothers who were also catchers. Gus Mancuso, brother of
Frank Mancuso, caught for the New York Giants in 1942,
1943 and 1944; Ray Hayworth, brother of Red Hayworth,
caught for the Brooklyn Dodgers in 1944 and 1945; and
Mike Garbark, New York Yankee catcher in 1944 and
1945, was the brother of Bob Garbark. In each case the
career of the catcher with the New York team ended in
1945, a war casualty of the healthy players' return.

> *What is the middle name of all three DiMaggio
> brothers?*

The middle name of all three DiMaggios—Joe, Dom and
Vince—is Paul. One other group of playing brothers
shared the same middle name, which was, in fact, their
last name. The Alou brothers all adopted their mother's
maiden name, "Alou," for baseball; their last name, which
became their middle name, was Rojas.

> *Name the players who played during all four decades
> of the Thirties, Forties, Fifties and Sixties.*

When "Minnie" Minoso took the field as the Chicago White Sox's designated hitter on September 11, 1976, he became the 14th man to play in four decades. Of those 14, three played in the Thirties, Forties, Fifties and Sixties—at least according to the record books. The three men identified by all the record books and guides as having spanned these four decades are Mickey Vernon, Ted Williams and Early Wynn. All three came up in 1939 and played until 1960, with Vernon and Williams retiring after the 1960 season and Wynn pitching into 1963 in quest of his 300th win.

But one other man came up in 1939 and because of a strange set of circumstances is not listed in the record books as having played that year, thus robbing him of the honor of having played in four decades. Elmer Valo was brought up in the closing weeks of the 1939 season by Connie Mack for an appraisal and sat on the Philadelphia A's bench game after game awaiting his chance. Finally, on the last day of the 1939 season, Mack sent him in as a pinch hitter and he walked. But a diligent scorekeeper pointed out to Mack that because the youngster hadn't officially been signed to a contract, the A's and Mack personally were subject to a fine at the hands of the commissioner, and requested permission to leave Valo out of the official score. Mack agreed with the scorekeeper, a relatively young writer out of Philadelphia named Red Smith, and Elmer Valo, who played through the 1960 season, was thus deprived of an opportunity for official trivia immortality.

The other 11 members of "The Four Decades Club" include Jim O'Rourke (1876–1904); Dan Brouthers (1879–1904); Jack O'Connor (1887–1910); William J. "Kid" Gleason (1888–1912); Deacon Jim McGuire (1884–1912); John B. Ryan (1889–1913); Eddie Collins

(1906–30); Nick Altrock (1898–1933); Jack Quinn (1909–33); Louis Norman "Bobo" Newsom (1929–53); and now, of course, Saturnino Orestes Minoso (Armas), or "Minnie" Minoso, as he's familiarly known, (1949–76).

### *Who was the only ballplayer born on February 29?*

The only player born on Leap Year's extra day was Johnny Leonard Roosevelt "Pepper" Martin, born on February 29, 1904, in Temple, Oklahoma. Nicknamed "The Wild Horse of the Osage," Pepper Martin came into the big leagues on a Leap Year, 1928, and closed out his major-league career in another Leap Year, 1944.

### *What player had his birthday on the back of his uniform?*

Bill Veeck is most often remembered as the man who introduced a midget into a major-league game (Eddie Gaedel, who appeared as a pinch hitter for Frank Saucier on August 19, 1951). But it was also Veeck who introduced one of the greatest aids for viewer involvement into the game—not to mention an aid for program sales—when he first put the names of the White Sox players on the backs of the uniforms (even purposely misspelling Ted Kluszewski's name as an attention getter). One member of the White Sox whose name appeared on his jersey was Carlos May, who joined the team long after Veeck's departure. May, one of only eight players whose names are also a month—all eight being May—wore number 17 under his name. His birthdate: May 17, 1948.

### *Who are the only three men to have their numbers retired twice?*

There have been 49 numbers retired by major-league clubs through the 1980 season, the latest one being number 20 on the St. Louis Cardinals, a tribute to Lou Brock, who ended his career after 16 years with the Cards. But two other men—Hank Aaron and Casey Stengel—had their numbers, 44 and 37, respectively, and respectfully, retired by the Atlanta Braves and Milwaukee Brewers and the New York Mets and New York Yankees.

One other player had his number retired twice, but neither time was it for him. New York Yankee outfielder Cliff Mapes was wearing number 3 when Babe Ruth made his farewell address at the 25th anniversary of Yankee Stadium on June 13, 1948. As a tribute to Ruth his number was retired that day—just the second time a man who had achieved greatness with his team was honored by having his number retired. Lou Gehrig's number 4 was the first time.

Mapes then took number 13 but soon switched over to number 7, the number he was wearing when a young shortstop named Mickey Mantle came up to the Yanks in 1951 wearing number 6. When Mapes was traded to Detroit later that year, his number was given to Mantle. When Mantle's number 7 was retired at a special "Mickey Mantle Day" in 1969, Mapes joined Stengel as one of the two men who had had their numbers retired twice.

## PERMANENTLY RETIRED UNIFORM NUMBERS

| AMERICAN LEAGUE | | NATIONAL LEAGUE | |
|---|---|---|---|
| No. | Club | No. | Club |
| | BALTIMORE | | ATLANTA |
| 5 | Brooks Robinson | 21 | Warren Spahn |
| 20 | Frank Robinson | 41 | Eddie Mathews |
| | | 44 | Hank Aaron |
| | BOSTON | | |
| 9 | Ted Williams | | CHICAGO—None |
| | | | CINCINNATI |
| | CALIFORNIA—None | 1 | Fred Hutchinson |
| | CHICAGO | | HOUSTON |
| 2 | Nellie Fox | 32 | Jim Umbricht |
| 4 | Luke Appling | 40 | Don Wilson |

| AMERICAN LEAGUE | NATIONAL LEAGUE |
|---|---|

| No. | Club | No. | Club |
|---|---|---|---|
| | **CLEVELAND** | | **LOS ANGELES** |
| 3 | Earl Averill | 4 | Duke Snider |
| 5 | Lou Boudreau | 19 | Junior Gilliam |
| 19 | Bob Feller | 24 | Walter Alston |
| | | 32 | Sandy Koufax |
| | **DETROIT** | 39 | Roy Campanella |
| 6 | Al Kaline | 42 | Jackie Robinson |
| | **KANSAS CITY—None** | | **MONTREAL—None** |
| | **MILWAUKEE** | | **NEW YORK** |
| 44 | Hank Aaron | 14 | Gil Hodges |
| | | 37 | Casey Stengel |
| | **MINNESOTA** | | |
| 3 | Harmon Killebrew | | **PHILADELPHIA** |
| 47 | Sherry Robertson | 1 | Richie Ashburn |
| | | 36 | Robin Roberts |
| | **NEW YORK** | | |
| 3 | Babe Ruth | | **PITTSBURGH** |
| 4 | Lou Gehrig | 1 | Bill Meyer |
| 5 | Joe DiMaggio | 20 | Pie Traynor |
| 7 | Mickey Mantle | 21 | Roberto Clemente |
| 8 | Bill Dickey-Yogi Berra | 33 | Honus Wagner |
| 15 | Thurmon Munson | | |
| 16 | Whitey Ford | | **ST. LOUIS** |
| 37 | Casey Stengel | 6 | Stan Musial |
| | | 17 | Dizzy Dean |
| | **OAKLAND—None** | 20 | Lou Brock |
| | | 45 | Bob Gibson |
| | **TEXAS—None** | | |
| | | | **SAN DIEGO—None** |
| | | | **SAN FRANCISCO** |
| | | 4 | Mel Ott |
| | | 11 | Carl Hubbell |
| | | 24 | Willie Mays |
| | | 27 | Juan Marichal |
| | | 44 | Willie McCovey |

*Who was the only player to play his entire major-league career for three teams, in three different leagues—all in one city?*

Last in the alphabetized listing in the Official Encyclopedia of Baseball, but first in the cities he played in for three different teams in three different leagues, is Edward "Dutch" Zwilling, who spent his entire career in the city of Chicago with the White Sox in the American League, the Whales in the Federal League and the Cubs in the National League in but four short years, ending in 1916. One other player, Rollie Zeider, also played for all three teams and in the same order that Zwilling played, but this three-time teammate of Zwilling's left the Windy City for 49 games with the Yankees in 1913 and spoiled his one-city record. Zwilling, the last man listed in the Encyclopedia of Baseball, shares one achievement with Hank Aaron, the first man listed: They both led their league in RBI's.

*In the order in which they were elected, name the first five players named to the Hall of Fame.*

When the Hall of Fame announced the results of the first vote ever for inclusion among 226 writers and players, these five greats were mentioned on over three-quarters of the ballots, insuring their election: Ty Cobb (with 222 votes); Babe Ruth and Honus Wagner (each received 215 votes); Christy Mathewson (205 votes); and Walter Johnson (189 votes).

*Who were the only three players to play for both the Milwaukee Braves and the Milwaukee Brewers?*

The Milwaukee Braves moved to Atlanta in 1966. The Seattle Pilots moved to Milwaukee to become the Milwaukee Brewers in 1970. And yet three players not only bridged the time span but also the difference in leagues to become members of both clubs. Those three were Hank Aaron, who played for the Milwaukee Braves from 1954 until they moved South and then rejoined the Brewers in 1975; Felipe Alou, who also moved South with the Braves in 1966 and then came back to join the Brewers in 1974; and Phil Roof, who played two games with the Braves, one in 1961 and again in 1964, and then caught for the entire 1970 and part of the 1971 season with the Milwaukee Brewers.

One other player claims both clubs, but only one as a player and the other as a manager. Del Crandall, the

Braves' longtime catcher, later became the manager of the Brewers, but did not play for both clubs.

*Who was the first regular player to "jump" to the newly formed Mexican League in 1946?*

New York Giants third baseman Nap Reyes was the first regular player to jump to the Mexican League in 1946, succumbing to the temptations that the Pascual brothers offered him to come to their new league. Other major-leaguers who jumped their contracts to join Reyes included Dodger catcher Mickey Owen, New York Giant outfielder Danny Gardella, Chicago White Sox pitcher Alex Carrasquel, Cardinal pitcher Max Lanier, Browns catcher Myron Hayworth, former Giant shortstop Frank Scalzi (who played under the name of "Rizutti" in Mexico), Senator outfielder Roberto Ortiz, New York Giants pitcher Sal Maglie, Brooklyn outfielder Luis Olmo, Phillies infielder Rene Monteagudo, A's outfielder Roberto Estelella, and Braves infielder Roland Gladu.

When the Mexican League folded and these unlucky 13 players sought reinstatement, Commissioner "Happy" Chandler refused to accept them and suspended all for five years. Only after Gardella sued baseball and forced the suspension to end in 1949 did a few of the 13 reenter major-league baseball, for the sum total of 887 games, with Maglie appearing in 290 more major-league games and turning in one no-hitter and a 20-game season. But most of the others weren't so lucky, including Gardella, who only came to bat one more time in the major leagues after his jump and reinstatement. He, like the Mexican League, failed to make a hit.

*Name the four major-league players whose last names are spelled the same backward as well as forward.*

A "palindrome" is defined as "a word, verse or sentence that is the same when read backward or forward." The most time-honored one is one that was attributed to Napoleon upon first sighting his place of exile: "Able was I ere I saw Elba." The four major-leaguers whose names are palindromes are Dick Nen of the Los Angeles Dodgers, Washington Senators and Chicago Cubs; Toby Harrah of the Washington Senators and Texas Rangers; Truck Hannah with the old New York Yankees; and Eddie Kazak of the St. Louis Cardinals and Cincinnati Reds. (Excluded from this list is Russ Van Atta, pitcher for the New York Yankees and St. Louis Browns. His last name is Van Atta, not just Atta. Emil Yde, pitcher for the Pittsburgh Pirates and Detroit Tigers, is also excluded. His name, though pronounced E-d-e, nonetheless is spelled in a nonreversible form.)

Added to these names is the playing palindrome, most notable of which is Warren Spahn's achievement of having won 363 games and also having 363 lifetime hits. (Read backward that's 363 hits and 363 games won.)

*Who had the longest complete name of any player who ever played in the majors?*

The longest name ever to appear in the Baseball Register is the name of a current player, the San Francisco Giants' third baseman, Al Gallagher, who also answers to his christened name Alan Mitchell Edward George Patrick Henry Gallagher, a handle with 45 letters in all. The name is a combination of all six boys' names that his father had saved up for a son. After waiting so long for a boy, he decided to use them all on Al.

Two other players come close. Bruno Betzel, an infielder with the St. Louis Cardinals from 1914 to 1918, was originally Christian Frederick Albert John Henry David Betzel, a total of 44 letters. And then there was the pitcher brought up in the Forties by the Dodgers who stayed around for 15 years and pitched for seven clubs. Called "Buster" for short, his entire moniker read Calvin Coolidge Julius Caesar Tuskahoma McLish, a total of 41 letters.

But even Alan Mitchell Edward George Patrick Henry Gallagher, the longest complete name of any player who ever played in the majors, cannot hold a candle to the longest name in movie history, 66 letters. The actor's full name was Rodolpho Pierre Filibert Alphanzo Rafael Gugliemi di Valentina d'Antoguella, but he was known simply as Rudolph Valentino.

*Who was the oldest player ever to appear in a major-league game?*

All of the oldest-player records belong, naturally, to that Methuselah of baseball, Leroy Robert "Satchel" Paige. Not only was Paige the oldest "rookie" ever to break into the majors (at the age of 42 in 1948), but he was also the oldest player ever to appear in a game in organized baseball, making a brief appearance for the Peninsula Club in the Carolina League at the age of 60 in 1966.

Born on July 7, 1906, he says, Satchel was 59 years and two months old at the time of his last major-league performance when, pitching for the Kansas City A's, he struck out one and allowed one hit and no runs in three innings. On that date he also became the oldest man ever to bat in a major-league game, going to bat and striking out. He thus eclipsed the record set by Nick Altrock on the last day of the 1933 season when Altrock, coaching for the Washington Senators, was inserted as a pinch hitter at the age of 57. Both thus top the "old-time" records held by George Blanda and Archie Moore in other sports. The records for performances by oldest players in each category follow:

## PERFORMANCES BY OLDEST PLAYERS

| Age (Years-Mos) | Performance by Oldest Player | Team | Date |
|---|---|---|---|
| 59-2 | Pitched—Satchel Paige | K.C. A's | 9/25/65 |
| 59-2 | Batted (0-1) Satchel Paige | K.C. A's | 9/25/65 |
| 52-1 | Caught—Jim O'Rourke | Giants | 9/20/04 |
| 53-9 | Hit (1-3) "Minnie" Minoso | White Sox | 9/12/76 |
| 47-11 | Double—Jack Quinn | Dodgers | 6/7/32 |
| 48-0 | Triple—Nick Altrock | Senators | 9/30/24 |
| 45-11 | Homer—Jack Quinn | Athletics | 6/7/30 |
| 41-5 | Grand Slam—Hans Wagner | Pirates | 7/29/15 |
| 52-11 | Scored Run—Charles O'Leary | Browns | 9/30/34 |
| 47-11 | RBI—Jack Quinn | Dodgers | 6/7/32 |
| 50-5 | Stolen Base—Arlie Latham | Giants | 8/18/09 |
| 45 | Play 100 Games (1B)—Cap Anson | Chi. N.L. | Season 1897 |
| 48-1 | Won Game (Relief)—Jack Quinn | Dodgers | 8/14/32 |
| 48-11 | Lost Game (Relief)—Jack Quinn | Reds | 6/28/33 |
| 46-2 | Pitched CG (won)—Satchel Paige | Browns | 9/20/52 |
| 46-2 | Shutout (4-0)—Satchel Paige | Browns | 9/20/52 |

*Who was the only MVP with two different teams in the same league?*

Almost everyone knows that Frank Robinson is the only man ever to win the Most Valuable Player Award in both the National and American Leagues, winning it while playing for Cincinnati in 1961 and for Baltimore in 1966. But how many know that since the Baseball Writers Association of America began selecting the Most Valuable Players, only one man, Jimmie Foxx, has ever won it playing for two different teams—in the same league? Foxx first won the MVP Award in the American League in 1932 as a member of the Philadelphia A's, repeated in 1933, again as a member of the A's, and then won it for the third time, in 1938, as a member of the Boston Red Sox.

*What future Hall of Famer was named after another member of the Hall of Fame?*

Born on October 20, 1931, the future Yankee great Mickey Mantle was christened Mickey Charles Mantle because his father was a fan of the then Philadelphia Athletics' catcher Gordon "Mickey" Cochrane.

*Name the player who was the second black to play in the American League and the first black to play for the New York Giants.*

Hank Thompson joined the St. Louis Browns in 1947, immediately after Larry Doby of the Indians had broken the color barrier in the American League, and played 27 games at second base, hitting .256. Thompson played in the Negro National League in 1948 and then joined the Giants' organization in 1949, playing first with Jersey City in the International League and then coming up to the Giants halfway through the season to play in 75 games at second and third bases and hit .280, the first black to play for the Giants.

*What number did Mickey Mantle wear when he came up to the Yankees? Yogi Berra? Joe Di-Maggio?*

Three of the most famous numbers in New York Yankee history, and in all of baseball, belonged to Mickey Mantle, Yogi Berra and Joe DiMaggio, and when each of them retired, so were their numbers. However, when they first came up, they had been assigned different numbers. Mantle came up in 1951 as a shortstop and was given the number 6 before receiving the number 7 he made famous. Berra came up in 1946 and originally wore number 35 before receiving number 8, which was still being worn at the beginning of the '46 season by Yankee catcher Bill Dickey. And Joe DiMaggio was originally assigned number 9 when he first came up in 1936, his future number, 5, being worn by another Yankee.

## 2ND INNING

# THE BATTERS

*Who was the first Latin American to win a batting title?*

Mexican-born Roberto Avila, with a .341 batting average in 1954, was the first Latin American to win a major-league batting championship. Avila, who won the title while playing for the Cleveland Indians, was but the first of several Latin Americans who have won the title, including Roberto Clemente, Matty Alou, Rico Carty, Rod Carew and Tony Oliva. The first ballplayer from Latin America to play in the "modern" major leagues was Louis Castro, a second baseman for the Philadelphia A's in 1902, who was born in Colombia.

*Who was the only man to pinch-hit for Ted Williams?*

Ted Williams played for 19 years and went to bat 7706 times, including 111 times himself as a pinch hitter. But in the very last week of his career in 1960, with his retirement at the season's end already announced, a pinch hitter was sent in to bat for "The Splendid Splinter," the only pinch hitter ever to bat for Williams in 19 years. The pinch hitter's name was Carroll Hardy, and he had come to bat six times before during the season as a pinch hitter and delivered twice. But this time he popped up into a double play, once more reinforcing the fact that nobody would ever replace "Terrible Ted."

*What batter holds the record for the most consecutive games without a strikeout?*

Little Jacob Nelson "Nellie" Fox went 98 consecutive games, from May 17 through August 22, 1958, without striking out, thereby setting the all-time record for consecutive games without striking out.

### Who was the first designated hitter?

Ron Blomberg of the New York Yankees became the American League's first designated hitter on April 6, 1973, when he appeared in the top of the first inning of the opening-day game against the Boston Red Sox in Fenway Park. Blomberg, batting sixth in the lineup, was assured his time at bat in the top of the first as the Yankees scored three runs. Thus, he came to bat before other designated hitters scheduled to hit that day for other teams playing in the American League.

The first home run by a designated hitter was hit later that same day by Tony Oliva of the Minnesota Twins.

### Who holds the record for the most homers hit in one month?

As July of 1937 turned into August, a young rookie rusted away on the Detroit Tigers' bench, wondering if he would ever make it into the Tiger lineup. The Most Valuable Player in the Texas League in 1935 and in the American Association in 1936, Rudy York had played at first and caught. But the Tigers needed little help at either position, with Hank Greenberg holding down first and player-manager Mickey Cochrane holding his own behind the plate. And so York was consigned to the bench.

When an opportunity to break into the lineup as a third baseman presented itself on August 4, after the Tigers had lost six straight games, York took advantage of the opportunity. He hit a home run in his first game in the regular lineup and went on to hit 18 in the month of August, an all-time one-month record, eclipsing the 17 Babe Ruth had hit in September of his 60-home-run year. He also batted in 49 runs, another one-month record, exceeding the best effort of Lou Gehrig, who had 48 RBI's in August of 1935.

York finished the year with 35 home runs and 103 RBI's, and although he played for 12 more years, he never reached 35 home runs again. No one, however, has ever approached his 18 home runs in one month.

*Name the only two men to drive in more than 100 runs in a season without hitting a home run.*

Whereas today's sluggers drive in more than 100 runs with many home runs and few hits, the "sluggers" in the dead ball era drove in runs without benefit of round-trippers. And two of them, Hughie Jennings in 1896 and Lave Cross in 1902, drove in 121 and 108 runs, respectively, without hitting a single homer. Jennings, a shortstop for the old Baltimore Orioles, batted .401, and Cross, a third baseman for the Philadelphia Athletics, batted .342, in accomplishing their feat.

The only "modern" hitters to drive in 100 runs without resorting to the long ball were Bill Sweeney of the Boston Braves, who in 1912 had 100 RBI's with only one homer; Ed Delahanty of the Philadelphia Phillies, who in 1900 had 109 RBI's with only two homers; and Billy Herman of the Brooklyn Dodgers, who drove in 100 runs in 1943 with only two home runs.

On the other side of the batting ledger, several "weak-hitting" batters have driven in 100 runs. The "leader" in the lowest-average 100 RBI's table is Roy Sievers, who hit just .232 in 1954 when he drove in 102 runs for the Washington Senators. Others who have batted under .250 and driven in over 100 RBI's include Harmon Killebrew, who hit .242 in 1959 and drove in 105 runs; Bob Allison, who drove in 105 runs in 1961 while batting just .245; Eddie Robinson, who batted .247 in 1953 and had 102 RBI's; and Jim Wynn, who batted .249 in 1967 with 107 RBI's.

*What modern player had the fewest home runs
in over 2000 at bats?*

Floyd Baker played for the St. Louis Browns, Chicago
White Sox, Washington Senators, Boston Red Sox and
Philadelphia Phillies for 13 years and went to bat
2280 times but hit only one home run.

In early 1949 Chicago White Sox General Manager
Frank Lane artificially shortened the fences at Comiskey Park to generate more home runs by his anemic-
hitting White Sox team. But when other teams took
a liking to the fences more than the White Sox, including the Washington Senators, who hit seven homers on May 3, 1949, Lane decided to tear the fences
down. Although the fence was torn down two days
after the Senators' splurge, it gave Floyd Baker one
extra day to bloop his only major-league home run
over it in over 2000 at bats.

*Name the player at each position who holds the
record for most home runs hit in a season. In
a lifetime.*

The nine players who hit the most home runs in one
year at their respective positions are some of the leading home-run hitters of all time, with one glaring
exception—Babe Ruth. For although Ruth had the
second highest one-season total, he played the same
position as the all-time leading home-run producer,
Roger Maris—right field. (It also should be noted
that Hank Greenberg is the all-time home-run hitter
at first base. Jimmie Foxx, who had the same number
of homers, 58 in 1932, played 13 games at third
base that year and hit a home run while a third baseman, thus giving him less than Greenberg *at first
base.)*

| | |
|---|---|
| 1B—Hank Greenberg | 58 in 1938 |
| 2B—Dave Johnson | 43 in 1973 |
| SS—Ernie Banks | 47 in 1958 |
| 3B—Eddie Mathews | 47 in 1953 |
| LF—Ralph Kiner | 54 in 1949 |
| CF—Hack Wilson | 56 in 1930 |
| RF—Roger Maris | 61 in 1961 |
| C —Johnny Bench | 45 in 1970 |
| P —Wes Ferrell | 9 in 1931 |

Most of the all-time position-by-position figures show many of the same names having the most career home runs, with Johnny Bench only recently having joined very exclusive company, surpassing Yogi Berra's previous career total of 313 as a catcher (and 358 overall). Upon learning of his having been surpassed in the all-time homer department, Yogi sent a telegram to Bench that read, in perfect Berra-ese, "I always knew my record would stand until it was broken." Some new names, however, appear, with Babe Ruth, Hank Aaron and Willie Mays replacing those of Roger Maris, Ralph Kiner and Hank Wilson, respectively. But again Jimmie Foxx, who hit 534 career homers, played almost 12 percent of his games at other positions, and therefore his home-run output as a *first baseman* falls below that of Lou Gehrig. Also, many of the lifetime home runs hit by those listed position-by-position were hit while they were playing positions *other* than the one for which they're listed. (For instance, Ernie Banks played 1125 games at shortstop, 1259 games at first and almost 100 games at other positions, hitting but 293 of his 512 homers as a shortstop.) Thus, for an accurate statistical position-by-position breakdown, the home runs hit at the position for the player follows the player's name; career homers in parentheses.

| | |
|---|---|
| 1B—Lou Gehrig | 493 |
| 2B—Rogers Hornsby | 264 (302) |

SS—Ernie Banks       293 (512)
3B—Eddie Mathews    482 (512)
LF—Hank Aaron      661 (755)
CF—Willie Mays      660
RF—Babe Ruth       692 (714)
C —Johnny Bench     356 (through 1980)
P —Wes Ferrell       36 ( 38)

*Who was the only slugger to hit more than 50 home runs in one year and yet strike out less than 50 times?*

Most home-run hitters, by the very nature of their from-the-heels swing, strike out a lot. In fact, every player who has hit 50 or more home runs has struck out more times than hit homers, with one exception— Johnny Mize. Mize hit 51 homers in 1947 to tie Ralph Kiner for the league lead, but only struck out 42 times. Two other home-run leaders—Lou Gehrig, who hit 49 homers to lead the American League in 1934, and Ted Kluszewski, who hit 49 in 1954 to lead the National League and hit 47 in 1955—also struck out fewer times than they hit homers. A list of those players who hit 47 or more homers in a season and the number of times they struck out follows:

### HOME RUNS PER SEASON VERSUS STRIKEOUTS

| Year | Player | HR | SO | Year | Player | HR | SO |
|---|---|---|---|---|---|---|---|
| 1961 | Roger Maris | 61* | 67 | 1954 | Ted Kluszewski | 49* | 35 |
| 1927 | Babe Ruth | 60* | 89* | 1962 | Willie Mays | 49* | 85 |
| 1921 | Babe Ruth | 59* | 81 | 1964 | Harmon Killebrew | 49* | 135 |
| 1932 | Jimmie Foxx | 58* | 96 | 1966 | Frank Robinson | 49* | 90 |
| 1938 | Hank Greenberg | 58* | 92 | 1969 | Harmon Killebrew | 49* | 84 |
| 1930 | Hack Wilson | 56* | 84* | 1933 | Jimmie Foxx | 48* | 93* |
| 1920 | Babe Ruth | 54* | 80 | 1962 | Harmon Killebrew | 48* | 142* |
| 1928 | Babe Ruth | 54* | 87* | 1969 | Frank Howard | 48 | 96 |
| 1949 | Ralph Kiner | 54* | 61 | 1971 | Willie Stargell | 48* | 154* |
| 1961 | Mickey Mantle | 54 | 112 | 1926 | Babe Ruth | 47* | 76 |
| 1956 | Mickey Mantle | 52* | 99 | 1927 | Lou Gehrig | 47 | 84 |
| 1965 | Willie Mays | 52* | 71 | 1950 | Ralph Kiner | 47* | 79 |
| 1947 | Ralph Kiner | 51* | 81 | 1953 | Eddie Mathews | 47* | 83 |
| 1947 | Johnny Mize | 51* | 42 | 1955 | Ted Kluszewski | 47* | 40 |
| 1955 | Willie Mays | 51* | 60 | 1958 | Ernie Banks | 47* | 87 |
| 1938 | Jimmie Foxx | 50 | 76 | 1964 | Willie Mays | 47* | 72 |
| 1930 | Babe Ruth | 49* | 61 | 1969 | Reggie Jackson | 47 | 142* |
| 1934 | Lou Gehrig | 49* | 31 | 1971 | Hank Aaron | 47 | 58 |
| 1936 | Lou Gehrig | 49* | 46 | | * League leaders | | |

*Who was the only left-hand-throwing, right-hand-hitting player to win a batting title?*

There have been very few left-hand-throwing, right-hand-hitting nonpitchers in organized baseball. The only one who ever won a batting title was Hal Chase, who won the title while playing first base for the Cincinnati Reds in 1916 with a .339 average, his highest mark in the majors. Other left-hand-throwing, right-hand-hitting nonpitchers include James E. Ryan, Patsy Donovan, Edward "Pop" Tate, John Cassidy and Warren Carpenter, all of whom played before the turn of the century, and Rube Bressler, Johnny Cooney, Paul Strand, Carl Warwick and Cleon Jones in modern times.

*What player hit into a triple play on his final at bat in the majors?*

On the final day of the 1962 season, playing against the Cubs in Wrigley Field, Mets catcher Joe Pignatano hit into a triple play which ended his six-year career on a rather negative and unique note.

*Who was the only catcher to win two batting titles?*

Only two catchers have ever won the batting championship, and one of those—Ernie Lombardi—won two titles, in 1938 with a .342 average, playing for Cincinnati, and in 1942 with a .330 average, catching for the Boston Braves. The only other catcher to capture a batting crown was Eugene "Bubbles" Hargrave, who batted .353 while catching for the Cincinnati Reds in 1926. But Hargrave, in winning his crown, went to bat only 326 times, fewer than the required number of at bats today.

*Who are the only three players to win the batting championship without hitting a home run?*

When Minnesota's Rod Carew won the second of his five batting championships in 1972 with a .318 average, he became the third player to win a batting crown without hitting a single home run. He had 170 hits in 535 at bats, with 21 doubles, 6 triples and no home runs, thus joining Pittsburgh's Ginger Beaumont, who hit .357 to lead the National League in 1902, and Brooklyn's Zack Wheat, who hit .335 to lead the National League in 1918, as the only batting leaders who didn't have a home run among their hits.

*What do Babe Ruth's 714th home run and Hank Aaron's 714th home run have in common?*

Both home runs were hit for the Braves——Ruth hitting his 714th on the afternoon of May 25, 1935, at Forbes Field off Pirate pitcher Guy Bush, and Aaron's 714th coming on April 4, 1975, at Riverfront Stadium off Cincinnati pitcher Jack Billingham.

*Who was the first man to hit 60 home runs in organized baseball?*

When Babe Ruth hit his 60th home run off Tom Zachary on September 30, 1927, he became the third man in the history of organized baseball to reach that mark. The previous year John Clabaugh of the Tyler, Texas, team in the East Texas League had hit 62. But it was Ruth's teammate, Tony Lazzeri, who first hit 60 home runs in organized ball, in 1925. Lazzeri had broken all the existing records not only for home runs but for runs batted in and runs scored in 1925, by hitting 60 home runs, scoring 202 runs and batting in 222 runs in 197 games——all records which still stand——while playing for the Salt Lake City team in the Pacific Coast League.

### PLAYERS WHO HAVE HIT 60 OR MORE HOME RUNS

| | | | | |
|---|---|---|---|---|
| 1925 | Tony Lazzeri | Salt Lake City | Pacific Coast League (AAA) | 60 |
| 1926 | John Clabaugh | Tyler | East Texas (D) | 62 |
| 1927 | Babe Ruth | New York | American | 60 |
| 1930 | Joe Hauser | Baltimore | International (AA) | 63 |
| 1933 | Joe Hauser | Minneapolis | Am. Association (AA) | 69 |
| 1948 | Bob Crues | Amarillo | West-Texas-New Mexico (C) | 69 |
| 1954 | Bob Lennon | Nashville | Southern Association (AA) | 64 |
| 1954 | Joe Bauman | Roswell | Longhorn (C) | 72 |
| 1956 | Ken Guettler | Shreveport | Texas (AA) | 62 |
| 1956 | Dick Stuart | Lincoln | Western (A) | 66 |
| 1961 | Roger Maris | New York | American | 61 |

*Who was the only player to hit eight home runs in one professional game?*

What? you say. *Eight* home runs? How is that possible? The record is four in one game. And you'd be right if we were confining ourselves to the major leagues. But on June 15, 1902, as Corsicana hosted Texarkana in a Texas League game, in an attempt to keep its winning streak alive, a 19-year-old catcher named Jay "Nig" Clarke went to bat eight times and immortalized his name by hitting eight balls out of the park, driving in 16 runs and hitting for 32 total bases, all professional records. Corsicana won a "squeaker" by a score of 51–3, as it went on to win 27 in a row—a record which still stands for all of organized baseball. That drove Texarkana out of the Texas League. They dropped out of the league in midseason, never to reenter it again.

As for Clarke, after each of his home runs the hat was passed for him and he garnered over $200, more than his yearly salary. He made it to the majors just three years later, where he stayed for nine years and amassed the sum total of six home runs in 1536 at bats, or two less than he had in one afternoon.

*Who was the youngest player ever to win a batting championship? The oldest?*

The youngest player to win a batting championship was Al Kaline, who in his second full season with the Detroit Tigers hit .340 to win the 1955 batting crown at the age of 20. The oldest player ever to win a batting championship was Ted Williams, who won the 1958 batting title with a .328 mark at the ripe old age of 40, 17 years after he had won his first batting championship with a .406 average in 1941.

*Who was the first player to make 3000 hits?*

There are only 12 players with 3000 or more hits. The first player to attain this plateau was Adrian "Cap" Anson, who had 3022 hits in a 22-year career that started in 1876 and ended in 1897. This pioneer member of the "3000-hit club" was later joined by Nap Lajoie, Honus Wagner, Ty Cobb, Tris Speaker, Eddie Collins, Paul Waner, Stan Musial, Willie Mays, Hank Aaron, Roberto Clemente and Al Kaline.

*What was the only year two men with the same last name led their respective leagues in the same batting category?*

The only time two men with the same last name led their leagues in a batting category was in 1962 when Frank Robinson of Cincinnati led the National League in doubles with 51 and Floyd Robinson of the White Sox led the American League with 45. Ironically, it was the only time Floyd was ever to lead the league in any department.

It also happened once in the pitching department when the White Sox's Clint Brown led the American League in saves with 18 and Pittsburgh's Mace Brown tied for the National League lead with 7.

*What brothers hold the combined record for the most home runs?*

For the answer, look no further than the first two names in the Official Baseball Encyclopedia, Hank and Tommie Aaron. For while Tommie had only ten in four years of play, Hank had 755 through 1976, for a combined total of 765, far ahead of the combined 573 total for the three DiMaggio brothers.

*What right-handed batter holds the record for most home runs in two consecutive seasons?*

Jimmie Foxx, the right-handed slugger who played most of his career for the Philadelphia A's and the Boston Red Sox, hit 58 home runs in 1932 and 48 in 1933 while playing for the A's, setting the all-time record for the most homers in two consecutive years for a right-handed batter—106. Babe Ruth hit 113 in two consecutive years, hitting 54 in 1920 and 59 in 1921.

*Who was the only modern player to lead the league in hits in each of his first three seasons in the majors?*

Johnny Pesky, who as John Paveskovich had been a clubhouse boy for the Portland Beavers of the Pacific Coast League, graduated to the majors in 1942 and led the majors in hits with 205—the only rookie to do so. (Even though Lloyd Waner had more hits—223— in his rookie year, he finished second to brother Paul.) Returning from two years in the military, Pesky again led the league in hits with 208 in 1946 and repeated in 1947 with a league-leading 207 hits, the only player to lead the league in hits in each of his first three years in the major leagues.

*What two future batting champions for the same team had exactly the same number of hits for an*

*American Association team the year before they came to the majors?*

Both Ted Williams and Carl Yastrzemski had 193 hits while playing with the Minneapolis Millers in the American Association the year before they were brought up by the Boston Red Sox. Yaz led the American Association in hits in 1960, the same year that Williams retired. Williams had had 193 hits while playing with Minneapolis in 1938 and led the American Association in batting with a .366 mark, in runs scored, total bases, home runs, runs batted in and bases on balls, but not, ironically, in hits.

*What is the record for the most times at bat in a season without a hit?*

In 1962 Bob Buhl, pitching for the Milwaukee Braves and the Chicago Cubs, went to bat 70 times without a hit, thus establishing the major-league record for all-time futility. But Buhl's ineffectiveness with the bat is matched by some other noted nonhitters like Dean Chance, Hank Aguirre and Hoyt Wilhelm, whose lifetime averages of .070, .081 and .088, respectively, are even lower than Buhl's .089.

*Name the only player to play in 60 or more games whose every hit one year was a home run.*

Clem Labine, pitcher for the Brooklyn and, later, Los Angeles Dodgers, came to bat 31 times in 60 games in 1955 and had but three hits—but every hit was a home run, giving him a home-run percentage of 9.7. (Babe Ruth's all-time lifetime mark is *only* 8.5 percent.)

*When Babe Ruth hit his 700th homer, only two men had as many as 300. Who were they?*

When Babe Ruth hit his 700th home run off Detroit pitcher Tommy Bridges in Navin Field on July 13, the only players who had as many as 300 home runs were Lou Gehrig with 314 and Rogers Hornsby with 301.

*Who was the youngest player ever to hit 50 or more home runs in one season in the majors? The oldest?*

The youngest player to hit 50 or more homers in one season was Willie Mays, who hit 51 in 1955 when he was 24. The oldest players to hit 50 or more homers are Willie Mays, who hit 52 homers in 1965, and Johnny Mize, who hit 51 homers in 1947, both at the age of 34.

*What player has broken up the most no-hitters by getting the only hit in the game?*

Cesar Tovar has broken up five different pitchers' bids for no-hitters, getting the only hit in a one-hit game. Tovar broke up the bids by Barry Moore and Dick Bosman of the Washington Senators, and Dave McNally and Mike Cuellar of the Orioles, as a member of the Minnesota Twins and Jim "Catfish" Hunter as a member of the Texas Rangers. Every one of Tovar's five "spoilers" was a single.

Billy Williams of the Chicago Cubs and Oakland A's has broken up five no-hit bids, but not once did he get just one hit, it was always at least two, and one time four hits.

Two other players have broken up four no-hitters: Ed Konetchy of the St. Louis Cardinals and Boston Braves, who broke up two no-hit bids in two consecutive games—June 28 and June 30, 1916—and Don Blasingame of the Cincinnati Reds and Washington Senators. And six players are credited with breaking up three no-hitters apiece with the only hits given up in the game: Sherry Magee, Harry Hooper, Bob Johnson, Del Ennis, Zoilo Versalles and Jim Northrup. But the most consistent "spoiler" of them all was Bobby Doerr, who broke up two of Bob Feller's no-hitters with the only hit, adding them to "Rapid Robert's" 11 one-hitters instead of his three no-hitters.

### Who hit the most lifetime home runs in Yankee Stadium?

The most lifetime home runs at Yankee Stadium were hit not by Babe Ruth but by Mickey Mantle, who hit 266 there during his 17-year career. Ruth hit 259 at Yankee Stadium and another 69 at the Polo Grounds, where the Yankees played during three of Ruth's most productive years—1920, 1921 and 1922. The all-time record for most home runs hit by one player in one park is Mel Ott's 323 at the Polo Grounds, which accounts for 63 percent of his lifetime 511 circuit blows.

### Who had the highest lifetime batting average in organized baseball?

Oscar "Ox" Eckhardt had 2783 hits in 7608 at bats, giving him a lifetime batting average of .366, just one point ahead of Ty Cobb's overall batting average of .365. What's that you say? Cobb's batting average was .367 and is in every book and enshrined at the Hall of Fame on his tablet?

True, but that was his major-league average *only*. When you combine his .367 in the majors with his minor-league average of just over .300, he falls just one point short of Eckhardt's total, compiled in 13 seasons, mostly in the minors. Eckhardt failed miserably in his two tryouts in the majors, collecting but ten hits in 52 times at bat for two second-division clubs. But his .367 average in the minors was no "fluke," with batting championships in the Texas League and the Pacific Coast League giving him impressive credentials. Eckhardt won the 1930 Texas League batting title with a .379 average and followed up by leading the Pacific Coast League in batting for four of the next five years with averages of .369, .371, .414 and .399. He hit .414 in 189 games in 1933, the highest in the history of the Pacific Coast League, and won the 1935 title by edging out Joe DiMaggio, .399 to .398, bunting safely twice on the last day of the season.

Eckhardt had an unusual, if not awkward, left-handed stance at the plate, which partially contributed to his nickname "Ox," as did his exploits with the NFL New York Giants, for whom he played halfback after his All-American days at the University of Texas.

*Who drove in the run that broke up baseball's only double no-hit game?*

Mention the name Jim Thorpe and some sports fans will remember his collegiate football days at Carlisle; it will revive some memories of him as the first president and star player of the embryonic National Football League; some will recall his decathlon win at the 1912 Olympics at Stockholm; and still others will have a faint remembrance that he was somehow associated with baseball. For Jim Thorpe was an all-round athlete, the greatest athlete of the 20th Century in a recent poll, and a man who could play all sports, including baseball.

But whatever legends surrounded Thorpe the athlete did not extend to Thorpe the baseball player. Brought up by the Giants, he never fulfilled the expectations that manager John McGraw once had for him, expectations that seemed only natural of a man proclaimed "The Greatest Athlete in the World." Instead, he labored through six uninspiring years in the majors, hitting .262 with merely seven homers and nursing a longing to return to his first love—football.

On the afternoon of May 2, 1917, at Chicago's Weeghman Park (now called Wrigley Field), Fred Toney of the Cincinnati Reds and Jim "Hippo" Vaughn of the Cubs had hooked up in the most classic pitching duel of all time—a double no-hitter. Toney put the Cubs down inning after inning without a hit, but the Reds were even less effective against the offerings of Vaughn with ten of them striking out through the first nine innings and none getting a hit. Then in the tenth inning with one out Larry Kopf of the Reds got the first hit of the game, a single, and, after Greasy Neale was retired, advanced to third when outfielder Cy Williams dropped Hal Chase's fly ball for a two-base error. Cincinnati's right fielder Jim Thorpe, recently acquired from the Giants, came to bat and topped Vaughn's offering just to the side of the mound, where Vaughn, retrieving the ball, found he could make no play on either the speedy Kopf racing in from third or the speedier Thorpe streaking to first.

Thus, the only double no-hit game in baseball history was broken up by the greatest athlete in the history of sports, Jim Thorpe.

*What ballplayer hit into the most triple plays in his career?*

The all-time leader for hitting into triple plays is Brooks Robinson of the Baltimore Orioles. Robinson, recently elected the all-time Oriole, hit into four in his career, proving he could do almost anything—even hit into triple plays—better than anyone else. His four were hit against Washington, Washington, Boston and Chicago.

### TRIPLE PLAYS HIT INTO BY BROOKS ROBINSON

| Date of Game | Opponents | Fielders and Positions | Inn. |
|---|---|---|---|
| June 2, 1958 | Wash. | Bridges (SS)-Becquer (1B) | 6 |
| Sep. 10, 1964 | Wash. | Kennedy (SS)-Blasingame (2B)-Cunningham (1B)-Brumley (C) | 5 |
| Aug. 18, 1965 | Bos. | Malzone (3B)-Mantilla (2B)-Horton (1B)-Malzone (3B) | 1 |
| Aug. 6, 1967 | Chi. | K. Boyer (3B)-Buford (2B)-McCraw (1B) | 5 |

## Who was the only man Stan Musial pitched to in the majors?

Most of those enshrined in Cooperstown once pitched in the majors. In fact, seven of the first eight inductees—Ty Cobb, Babe Ruth, Honus Wagner, Christy Mathewson, Walter Johnson, Tris Speaker and Cy Young—pitched at least one game in the major leagues. But whereas most of those players did not actively pitch in the minors, one Hall of Famer, Stan Musial did. Musial won six games in his first year in the minors for Williamson (West Virginia) in the Mountain States Class D League and came back the next year to win nine of his 11 decisions for Williamson. The Cardinals then transferred his contract to Daytona Beach of the Florida State League, where he won 18 and lost just five for them in 1940 for an overall minor-league record of 33 wins and 13 losses.

Then something happened to his arm, and no matter what therapy Musial tried nor what advice his manager, Dickie Kerr (the same Dickie Kerr who won two games in the 1919 World Series for the "Black Sox"), gave, it was obvious his career as a pitcher was through. Staying at Kerr's house during the winter of 1940–41 gave Stan much time for soul-searching, and together he and Kerr decided that although his arm was gone, his bat was not. His .311 average in 1940 as a pitcher and part-time outfielder clearly indicated that he could make it on the strength of his hitting alone. The rest was history, seven batting championships, five times leading the league in hits, eight times in doubles, five times in triples, six times in slugging average and the Hall of Fame in 1969.

But for one moment, as part of a late-season stunt, the Cardinal management allowed Musial to take the mound and pitch to one major-league batter. And so on the last day of the 1952 season at Sportsman's Park in St. Louis, with the Cards 9½ games back of the Brooklyn Dodgers, Stan Musial went out to pitch to Chicago Cubs' outfielder Frankie Baumholtz. As the left-handed Musial stepped on the rubber, the usually left-handed-hitting Baumholtz stepped to the right side of the plate for the first time in his career. He hit the pitch down to Billy Johnson at third, who participated in the festivities by fumbling it away for an error. And so Musial's big-league pitching record shows no hits allowed, no runs allowed and one pitch thrown.

*What was the only year that there was a Triple Crown winner in both the American and National leagues?*

There have been 13 Triple Crown winners, starting with Ty Cobb in 1909 through Carl Yastrzemski in 1967, and won eight times in the American League and but five in the National. But only in 1933 were there winners in each league—and in the same city: Jimmie Foxx of the A's won the American League Triple Crown with 48 home runs, 163 RBI's and a .356 batting average, and Chuck Klein of the Phillies won the National League Triple Crown with 28 home runs, 120 RBI's and a .368 average.

There was one other time when there were two

Triple Crown winners in the same year, 1937. But this question is a horse of a different color, with the two winners being baseball's Joe Medwick of the St. Louis Cardinals (.374 BA, 31 homers and 154 RBI's) and War Admiral (the Kentucky Derby, the Preakness and the Belmont Stakes).

*What team's outfield combination had the highest single-season batting average?*

The 1894 Philadelphia Phillies outfield numbered no less than four .400 hitters. Left fielder Ed Delahanty batted .407, center fielder Billy Hamilton hit .404, and right fielder Sam Thompson hit at a .407 clip. A fourth outfielder, Tuck Turner, surpassed all of them with a .416 mark. This outfield combination, or "foursome," collectively hit .408 and finished 2-3-3-5 in the batting-championship standings. And the Phillies? They managed to finish in fourth place in the National League, 18 games behind the first-place Baltimore Orioles.

*Name the only five men to have 200 or more hits in a season and not hit .300.*

The 200-hit level has been one of those magical marks that statisticians and writers make note of and players strive to attain. Theoretically, its attainment will assure the player of having a good batting average, as when Babe Ruth had exactly 200 hits in 1924 and led the league in batting with a .378 average. But there have been four times when batters—all National Leaguers—had 200 or more safeties and yet failed to reach the .300 level: Jo-Jo Moore of the New York Giants in 1935 had 201 hits and a .295 batting average; Maury Wills of the Los Angeles

Dodgers in 1962 had 208 hits and a .299 average; Lou Brock of the St. Louis Cardinals had 206 hits in 1967 but only a .299 average; Matty Alou of the Pittsburgh Pirates had 201 hits in 1970 and only hit .297; and Buddy Bell of the Texas Rangers had exactly 200 hits in 1979 and had a .299 batting average.

*What player won the batting title and was disqualified under the then-existing rules?*

Before the rule change in 1951 requiring 400 times at bat to qualify for the batting title, the rule required only that the player appear in 100 games. However, the American League office disqualified Washington's Taffy Wright in 1938, although he had met the prerequisite of appearing in 100 games. Wright appeared in exactly 100 games in his first year in the majors, coming to bat only 263 times and getting 92 hits for a .350 average. Instead, the league ruled that even under the existing rules Wright had not come to bat enough times and ruled that the 1938 batting champion was Jimmie Foxx, who had a .349 batting average in 149 games, with 565 at bats and 197 hits.

The rule requiring 400 times at bat (since changed to 502 plate appearances, including walks and sacrifices) also deprived a potential batting champion of his crown. In 1954 Ted Williams officially came to bat only 386 times, walking another 136 times to lead the league in that category. But because he had not come to bat officially 400 times, he was disqualified from winning the batting title, which went to Roberto Avila with a .341 average, four points lower than Williams's.

*What major-league player hit a home run his first time at bat in the majors and didn't hit another homer in his next 21 years of play?*

More than 30 players have hit home runs their first times up in the majors. The first time it was ever done, on April 21, 1898, it was a pitcher, "Frosty" Bill Duggleby of the Philadelphia National League team, who did it—a grand-slam homer no less. But the most noteworthy of all of those who hit homers their first time up was the blow struck by Hoyt Wilhelm. On April 23, 1952, pitching in relief for the defending National League champion Giants, Wilhelm hit one into the left-field stands at New York's Polo Grounds, a feat he would never accomplish again in 21 years and almost 500 at bats in the majors.

*Who were the only two players to hit pitch-hit grand-slam homers in each league?*

There have been over 120 pinch-hit grand-slam home runs hit in major-league history, but only two men have hit them in each league. The first one was Jimmie Foxx, who hit one for the Philadelphia A's on September 21, 1931, off Tommy Bridges of the Detroit Tigers, and one on May 18, 1945, as a member of the Philadelphia Phillies, off Ken Burkhart of the Cardinals. The other man to hit a grand-slam pinch homer in each league was Roy Sievers, who hit one as a member of the same Philadelphia Phillies on May 26, 1963, against Bill Henry of Cincinnati, and also hit one in the American League on June 21, 1961, as a Chicago White Sox off Don Mossi of the Indians.

*Who led his league in singles the most times?*

Ralph Kiner was fond of saying that "home-run hitters drive Cadillacs, but singles hitters drive Fords." If this is the case then the late Nellie Fox must have owned a fleet of Fords, for he led the American League in singles eight times and the last seven times in a row, from 1954 through 1960. Ty Cobb led the American League six times, and Roger Cramer five times. Richie Ashburn, Maury Wills and Ginger Beaumont led the National League four times. But Nellie Fox cornered the market on Fords, leading the league a record eight times, as 2161 of his 2663 hits were singles.

*Who were the only two hitters to lead their league in singles, doubles and triples in the same year?*

Only Ty Cobb in 1911 and Stan Musial in 1946 led their respective leagues in singles, doubles and triples in the same year. Cobb also led the American League in batting, hits, total bases, runs batted in, slugging average and runs scored in 1911, but failed by one homer to sweep every batting category, hitting eight to "Home Run" Baker's nine. Musial nearly duplicated Cobb's feat in 1946, winning the batting crown and leading the league in total bases, slugging average, runs scored and hits, but trailing Ralph Kiner by seven in the race for home-run honors, 23 to 16, and coming in third in RBI's with 103 to teammate Enos Slaughter's 130.

*What brother combination had the most base hits?*

There have been many brother combinations, the five Delahanty brothers, the four O'Neill brothers, the three Alou brothers and the three DiMaggio brothers among them. But the brother combination that had the most hits in the majors was the Waners, Paul and Lloyd, who between them had 5611 hits in 38 years of combined play. Paul, one of 11 players to pass the 3000-hit mark, had 3152 hits, and his younger brother, "Little Poison," had 2459 hits. The Alous —Matty, Jesus and Felipe—playing from 1958 through 1975, amassed *just* 5038 hits, 573 short of the Waners' record.

*Name the modern player who holds the record for most total bases by a lead-off man in one game.*

When Davey Lopes of the Los Angeles Dodgers hit three homers, a double and a single on August 20, 1974, against the Chicago Cubs (thanks to a generous wind), he set a modern record for most total bases for a lead-off man with 15. The one-game splurge was the best ever by a National League second baseman, and doubled Lopes's 1974 home-run total to six.

The major-league record for most total bases in a game belongs to Joe Adcock, who on the afternoon of July 31, 1954, hit four home runs and one double for 18 total bases. Gil Hodges had 17 total bases on the night of August 31, 1950, when he hit his four homers together with one single. The American League record is 16, set by Ty Cobb in 1925 and tied in 1975 by Boston's Freddie Lynn, who had three home runs, one triple and one single. And Rennie Stennett, the first modern player to have seven hits in one game? He had only 11 total bases for his seven hits—four singles, two doubles and one triple.

*Name the only player to hit two home runs in his first two times up in the majors.*

On September 14, 1951, a husky outfielder named

Bob Neiman, just brought up by the St. Louis Browns from their Oklahoma City farm team, hit two of Boston Red Sox pitcher Maury McDermott's left-handed offerings over the Fenway Park "Green Monster" in his first two times at bat in the major leagues—the only player to hit two homers in his first two times at the plate. The only other player to hit two home runs in his first game was Bert Campaneris, but his came in his first and third times at bat, not quite matching Neiman's feat of hitting two in his first two at bats.

*Who was the only batter in major-league history to be called out for "refusing to bat"?*

Amos Rusie, an overpowering farmboy from Indiana, was one of the National League's stellar pitchers before the turn of the century. During his ten-year career with the New York Giants, he won 245 games, including 20 in four seasons and 30 in four straight seasons.

But just as his pitches were overpowering, his pride was more so. Rusie, who would ultimately hold out for a higher salary for three years at the very height of his career, would refuse to do what didn't suit him. And apparently it didn't suit him to bat on the afternoon of August 22, 1891, in a game against the Philadelphia National League club. So umpire Tim Hurst had no other recourse than to rule Rusie out.

The incident appears in a cryptic notation in the box score to explain why Philadelphia only had 26 putouts: "Rusie declared out for refusing to bat."

This great pitcher who was to go on to win 33 games that year, added one more footnote to baseball history. After his two-year holdout, he was traded by New York to Cincinnati in 1901 for a young, untried pitcher named Christie Mathewson. Rusie appeared in just three games for the Reds, winning none and losing one before calling it quits. Mathewson won 367 games for his new club.

*What player ran around the bases backward to commemorate his 100th home run?*

On June 23, 1963, Jimmy Piersall of the New York Mets hit a homer over the Polo Grounds' wall for his 100th home run in the majors and then ran around the bases backward to commemorate a feat that had taken him 13 years to accomplish, prompting baseball to issue a rule that no one could run the bases backward again.

# 3RD INNING

# THE PITCHERS

*Name the only pitcher to lead his league in ERA with an eighth-place team.*

Only Bob Friend of the Pittsburgh Pirates led his league in ERA while with an eighth-place team. Friend won 14 and lost 9 for the 1955 Pirates, compiling a league-leading 2.83 ERA while pitching for the tail-enders. One other pitcher, Steve Carlton of the 1972 Philadelphia Phillies, has led the league in ERA while with a "last-place" team, but the hapless Phillies of '72 were *only* a sixth-place team, even if their 59-97 won-lost record was worse than the Pirate̶s̶ ̶1̶9̶5̶5̶...

*What pitcher won 19 games more times than any other pitcher?*

Although the magic number of wins for pitchers is 20, Jim Bunning won 19 four times—one more time than Cy Young—including three seasons in a row when he just couldn't break into the charmed circle of 20 wins. One of those seasons was 1964, when his 20th win would have meant the pennant to the Phillies, who lost ten of their last 11 games and the pennant.

*Who was the only pitcher to win 20 games in a single season, split between two leagues?*

When the Yankees waived Hank Borowy out of the American League because he wasn't "a second-half pitcher" and sold him to the Chicago Cubs midway through the 1945 season, Borowy already had won ten games and lost five. He quickly fit into the Cubs' starting rotation and won 11 of his 13 decisions to propel the Cubs to a three-game margin of victory over the pursuing Cardinals. Borowy thus became the only pitcher to win 20 games split between the two leagues, his only 20-game season and the Cubs' last pennant win.

Five other pitchers attained the magic total of 20 or more wins pitching for two clubs—but all in the same league. Bobo Newsom won 20 between St. Louis and Detroit in 1939; Virgil Trucks won 20 between St. Louis and Chicago in 1953; "Red" Barrett won 23 in 1945 between Boston and St. Louis (NL); Jack Taylor won 20 between St. Louis and Chicago (NL) in 1906; and Bob Wicker won 20 between St. Louis and Chicago (NL) in 1903. But only one man—Borowy—could split his wins between two clubs in different leagues.

Name the only one-legged pitcher ever to pitch in the majors.

Although every baseball fan either saw *The Monty Stratton Story* or has read about Stratton's valiant attempts at a comeback after his tragedy, he never pitched in a major-league game after he lost his leg in a hunting accident. But one of those wounded World War II veterans who returned to the baseball scene, Bert Shepherd, did.

Shepherd had been a brilliant left-hander before the war and enlisted immediately after December 7, 1941, as an aviation cadet. He won his wings, rose to first lieutenant and flew several combat missions over Germany and France. It was on just such a mission that his plane was shot down over France and his right leg severely injured. The Germans tried to treat it and wound up amputating the leg.

Liberated by Patton's victorious armies, Shepherd returned to what he knew best, baseball. Fitted with an artificial limb, he requested a tryout with Washington and was accepted by the talent-starved Senators. He was the sensation of the training camp, fielding bunts and running to cover first as well as any pitcher Washington had. He even pitched and won an exhibition game against Brooklyn, with Durocher threatening any Dodger who bunted on him with a fine of $500. When the season opened, the Senators' team started to jell and Shepherd was pressed to find a spot on the club. But he did get into one game that year before he was released, pitching five innings and giving up only three hits, one run and one base on balls while striking out two.

*Name the only pitchers to throw no-hitters in their first major-league starts.*

Only three pitchers—Ted Breitenstein, "Bumpus" Jones and Bobo Holloman—have thrown no-hitters in their first starts. Breitenstein, the only man to throw no-hitters at both the old distance of 50 feet and the current distance of 60 feet, 6 inches, pitched a no-hitter in his first start. Charles "Bumpus" Jones pitched a no-hitter on October 15, 1892, the latest no-hitter in history, in his first start. And Alva "Bobo" Holloman pitched a no-hitter on May 6, 1953, in his first start and only complete game in the major leagues.

One other rookie, Charley Robertson of the Chicago White Sox, pitched a perfect game on April 30, 1922, in his third major-league start, setting the hard-hitting Detroit Tigers, who were to bat .305 as a team that year, down without a man reaching first.

*Who was the youngest pitcher ever to throw a no-hitter? The oldest?*

Oakland A's pitcher Vida Blue, who came into the big leagues briefly in 1969 and 1970, threw a no-hitter on September 21, 1970, and at the tender age of 21 years and 3 months, became the youngest pitcher ever to hurl a no-hit game.

The oldest ever to throw a no-hitter was the aptly named "Old" Cy Young, who pitched his third no-hitter against the New York Highlanders on June 30, 1908, at the ripe old age of 41 years and 3 months. Young, who didn't throw the first of his 77 shutouts until his third full year in the majors, was a "late bloomer," throwing his first no-hitter in his eighth year, at the age of 30, his second—a perfect game—at the age of 37, and his last one at the age of 41, three full years before he retired.

### Who threw the "Epheus" pitch?

The "Epheus" pitch was Truett "Rip" Sewell's own version of the blooper ball, which he threw on several occasions during his 13-year career with the Pittsburgh Pirates. Perhaps the pitch gained more attention for being hit than it ever did for befuddling the hitters, as it had for so many years.

During the eighth inning of the 1946 All-Star game, Sewell had come in to pitch for the National League, which was then in the process of being beaten 8–0 by the American League. Sewell was greeted by singles off the bats of Snuffy Stirnweiss and pitcher Jack Kramer, and after a sacrifice fly by Sam Chapman brought the ninth run home, he decided to regale his opponents with his famed Epheus pitch. First Vern Stephens sliced it to center for a single, and then Ted Williams, moving up a step in the batter's box to time its downward trajectory, unloaded on one that went sailing high into the right-field bleachers of familiar Fenway Park for a three-run homer.

Bobo Newsom had his blooper and Steve Hamilton his "Folly Floater," but none could touch Rip Sewell's "Epheus." Unless it was Ted Williams.

### What pitcher hit the most batsmen in the 20th Century?

Although he proclaimed that he was afraid to hit anyone with his blazing fast ball, Walter Johnson managed to

hit 206 opposing hitters who had dug in waiting for the
only pitch Johnson had. Leading the league in hit batsmen only once, Johnson, like any great pitcher, had his
wild moments, once throwing four wild pitches in one
inning for a negative record. Chick Fraser, a side-armer
who pitched from 1896 through 1909, holds the all-time
record with 215 hit batsmen, but several of them, including 28 in his rookie 1896 season, were 19th-Century victims. Only two pitchers in recent years have hit more than
100 batters in their careers—Don Drysdale with 154
hit batsmen, the modern National League record, and Jim
Bunning with 160, in both leagues. The 15 leading pitchers in the All-Time Hit Parade are as follows:

### ALL-TIME LEADERS IN HIT BATSMEN

| Hurler | Hit Batters | Innings Pitched |
|---|---|---|
| Charles Fraser | 215 | 3356 |
| Walter Johnson | 206 | 5924 |
| Eddie Plank | 188 | 4505 |
| Joe McGinnity | 184 | 3441 |
| Jim Bunning | 160 | 3759 |
| Don Drysdale | 154 | 3432 |
| Howard Ehmke | 137 | 2821 |
| George Dauss | 121 | 3391 |
| Jack Warhop | 114 | 1424 |
| George Uhle | 113 | 3120 |
| Jack Chesbro | 109 | 2897 |
| Urban Faber | 104 | 4088 |
| Tom Hughes | 101 | 2644 |
| Earl Whitehill | 101 | 3566 |
| Wilbur Cooper | 100 | 3480 |

*Name the only clubs that had four 20-game win-
ners. Four 20-game losers.*

The only two clubs to have four 20-game winners on
their staffs were the 1920 Chicago Black Sox (with Red
Faber, Claude Williams, Dickie Kerr and Eddie Cicotte
winning 87 games between them) and the 1971 Baltimore
Orioles (with Dave McNally, Pat Dobson, Mike Cuellar
and Jim Palmer winning 81 games between them). The

Sox finished second and the Orioles lost the Series to Pittsburgh, despite their pitching.

On the negative side, the only three teams to have four 20-game losers on their staffs were the 1905 and 1906 Boston Braves and the 1908 Brooklyn Dodgers. The Braves' 1905 pitching staff consisted of Irv Young, Chick Fraser, Vic Willis and Kaiser Wilhelm, who lost 94 games between them. The 1906 staff bettered that with Irv Young (suffering through the second of his three consecutive 20-game losing seasons, another negative record), Jeff Pfeffer, Gus Dorner and Vive Lindaman combining to lose a total of 95 games between them. The 1908 Dodgers had three 20-game losers in Nap Rucker, Harry McIntire and Jim Pastorius and the "ace" of the staff, Kaiser Wilhelm (who had learned the "art of losing" with the Braves), with 21 losses for a grand total of 81 between them. Ironically, only the 1906 Braves finished in last place, the 1905 Braves and the 1908 Dodgers finishing in seventh—but not because of their pitching.

*What pitcher struck out the most batters in organized ball?*

The answer, surprisingly, is Jim Bunning. Bunning, who pitched in the majors from 1955 through 1971, struck out 2855 in the major leagues, which places him behind Walter Johnson's 3499. But Bunning's 788 strikeouts in minor-league ball, combined with his 2855, moves him to the top of the strikeout list over Johnson, who pitched to only one batter in the minors while managing Newark in 1928, walking him.

*Who was the only pitcher to be named Rookie of the Year, Most Valuable Player and Cy Young Award winner?*

Only Don Newcombe of the Brooklyn Dodgers has won all three major awards—Rookie of the Year, Most Valuable Player and Cy Young Award. "Newk" won the National League's very first Rookie of the Year Award in 1949 when he won 17 and lost eight. He later won both the Most Valuable Player and Cy Young awards in 1956 (again the first recipient of the National League's Cy Young Award) when he posted a record of 27 wins and just seven losses to lead the league in wins and in winning percentage—and the Dodgers to the pennant.

Tom Seaver is the only other pitcher who has ever won the Rookie of the Year honor and gone on to win the coveted Cy Young Award, but Seaver has never been named MVP. And Sandy Koufax, Vida Blue, Denny McLain and Bob Gibson both won the MVP and Cy Young awards, but neither had been Rookie of the Year.

*Name the game in which the two pitchers were the tallest winning and losing pitchers in major-league history.*

Although pitcher Eppa Rixey is the tallest player in the Hall of Fame at 6'5" and Johnny Gee, who pitched for the Pittsburgh Pirates and the New York Giants between 1939 and 1946, was the tallest pitcher ever to take the mound in a major-league game, at 6'9", none of his 19 career decisions (seven wins and 12 losses) were against another pitcher of commensurate proportions. The game in which the tallest winning and losing pitchers took part was the 1955 All-Star game in Milwaukee. In that 12-inning classic, Milwaukee's hometown hero, 6'8" Gene Conley, came out to pitch to the American League in the top of the 12th and struck out Al Kaline, Mickey Vernon and Al Rosen in succession. In the bottom of the 12th, the first pitch from Frank Sullivan, the 6'7" Boston Red Sox righthander, to Stan Musial ended up in County Stadium's right-field bleachers, making Sullivan the tallest losing and

Conley the tallest winning pitcher in major-league history. Ironically, five years later, after the 1960 season, the Boston Red Sox traded the same Frank Sullivan to the Philadelphia Phillies for the same Gene Conley—the two tallest players ever in a trade.

*Who was the only ambidextrous pitcher to pitch in the majors?*

The only pitcher who pitched both left-handed and right-handed in the majors was Tony Mullane, who pitched for eight clubs between 1881 and 1894. Mullane, who alternated continually during his pitching stint to confuse the opposition, must have been very successful with his maneuver, as he won 285 games in the process, including five straight 30-game seasons. No modern pitcher ever threw both left-handed and right-handed in an official game. Dave "Boo" Ferriss of the Boston Red Sox used to warm up by pitching alternately with his left and right hands and had pitched with both in the minors. And so had Bert Campaneris, the talented Oakland A's shortstop, when he pitched for Daytona Beach in the Florida State League, as did Paul Richards, who became better known as a major-league manager than as an ambidextrous pitcher for Muskogee in the Western Association in 1928.

*Who was the first modern pitcher to relieve himself on the mound?*

This question can be misinterpreted in much the same way as an old historical marker on the road between Washington, D.C., and Richmond, Virginia, which read "Lee's Last Movement." But with relief pitching a vital part of every game and where very few starting pitchers ever go the complete route, the variations of relief pitching are immense, even the possibility that a pitcher could relieve himself or, rephrased, provide relief help for himself. Paul Richards, manager of the Chicago White Sox, first stage-managed a change of positions so that a pitcher could, in fact, relieve himself (while also relieving his reliever).

On May 15, 1951, at Boston's Fenway Park, White Sox pitcher Harry Dorish was working in relief in the bottom of the ninth. The first scheduled batter was Ted Williams, a left-handed batter who would be facing the right-handed Dorish. Richards called time and waved in left-hander Billy Pierce to pitch to Williams, moving Dorish to third base and taking the third baseman out. Pierce retired Williams and was removed, with Dorish coming back in to pitch to Boston's cleanup man as a new third baseman came into the lineup. Dorish wound up winning 9–7 in 11 innings, making modern history as the first man to ever relieve himself on the mound.

Stimulated by his success in this maneuver to relieve relief pitchers, Richards pulled it three more times: once in 1953, moving left-handed pitcher Billy Pierce to first and bringing him back to relieve himself after his own reliever had pitched to one batter; and two more times in 1954, when he moved right-handed Sandy Consuegra to third for one batter and then moved him back to the mound, and in another game moved left-handed Jack Harshman over to first for one batter and then brought him back to relieve himself.

*Who was the only pitcher to strike out 300 or more batters and not lead his league in strikeouts?*

Oakland A's pitcher Vida Blue struck out 301 men in 1971 while on his way to 24 wins, the lowest ERA in the American League and the MVP and Cy Young awards. But that was the year Detroit's Mickey Lolich put together a record of 25 wins and 308 strikeouts to lead the league in both categories.

*Who was the only pitcher to hit a pinch-hit grand-slam home run and also to serve one up?*

Early Wynn played 23 years in the majors and was called upon to pinch-hit 90 times. In 1946 he pinch-hit six times, getting three hits and one grand-slam home run— on September 15 against Jack Gorsica of the Tigers. Then, 15 years later, on May 28, 1961, pitching for the Chicago White Sox, Wynn served up one to the Yankees' Bob Cerv, making him the only pitcher ever to hit a pinch-hit grand slammer and also to pitch one.

*Name the pitcher off whom Babe Ruth hit his first major-league home run. His last.*

On May 6, 1915, in his 18th major-league at bat, Babe Ruth led off the third inning against the New York Yankees' right-handed submariner Jack Warhop. He jumped on the first pitch and sent it out of the park, the first of his 714 major-league homers. Down through the years Ruth hit many famous home runs off many pitchers, hitting 12 off Howard Ehmke, ten off George Earnshaw and nine each off Walter Johnson and Tom Zachary, including his 60th home run in 1927.

His most famous home run was his "called shot" in the 1932 World Series against the Cubs. Riding the Cubs unmercifully for giving former teammate Mark Koenig only one-half a Series share after he had joined them late in the year and for leaving former manager Rogers Hornsby out altogether, although he had managed them for over three-fifths of the season, Ruth was subjected to the Cubs' abuse and the fans' garbage. In the third game —the first in Chicago—Ruth hit a homer in the first off Charlie Root to give the Yankees a short-lived 3–1 lead. Coming to the plate in the fifth, he responded to the boos and lemons thrown from the stands by pointing to the center-field bleachers and, with the count two strikes and one ball, hitting one of the longest homers ever seen in Chicago, or anywhere.

Three years later, his career near an end, Ruth had one more Ruthian moment in Pittsburgh when, as a member of the Boston Braves, he hit his last three home runs, the first man to hit three in each league. His first was hit off Red Lucas and his last two off Guy Bush, who had lost to the Yankees as a member of the Cubs in the 1932 Series. But even with the three homers, the Braves lost, 11–7, and the winning pitcher was another familiar name, Ruth's ex-teammate Waite Hoyt, who was now pitching for the Pirates.

### What pitcher gave up the most bases on balls in the history of organized baseball?

Think of bases on balls and you'll think of Early Wynn, who issued the most in the majors with 1775, or Bob Feller with 1764. But the man who gave up more free passes than either of these two was Louis Norman "Bobo" Newsom, who walked 1732 in his 20-year major-league career and another 898 in the minors for the all-time record of 2630 walks in organized baseball. Newsom was also one of two 200-game winners to lose more than he won—the other, Jack Powell.

### Who hit Ray Chapman?

The only player to die on the ball field was Ray Chapman, star shortstop for the pennant-bound Cleveland Indians. Chapman was hit in the head by a pitch thrown by submariner Carl Mays on August 16, 1920, at the Polo Grounds. Leading off the top of the fifth inning, Chapman was hit on the left side of the head by the first ball thrown by Mays. So sharp was the report of the impact against his head that most people in the stadium, including pitcher Mays, who fielded the ball which had rebounded halfway to the pitcher's mound, believed

Chapman had hit it. The fatally injured Chapman slumped to the ground, where he was helped by teammates who lifted him to his feet. After a few steps his legs crumpled under him and Chapman fell to the ground, never to regain consciousness. He died the next morning after a last-minute operation to alleviate intercranial pressure.

At a loss for someone to replace their fancy-fielding shortstop, who was batting .303 at the time of his death, the Indians tried an outfielder, Joe Evans, at short, then second baseman Harry Lunte, and finally brought up little Joe Sewell. Sewell filled in admirably, hitting .329 for the rest of the 1920 season and staying in the majors for 13 more years, hitting .312 over the course of his career and striking out only 114 times, or eight times a season.

The only other near-tragic beaning occurred on May 25, 1937, at Yankee Stadium when Bump Hadley, pitching again for New York, hit Detroit's playing manager Mickey Cochrane, again in the fifth inning, fracturing his skull, although not as severely as Chapman's. This was the last game that Cochrane, batting just four percentage points higher than Chapman had been when he was hit, ever played.

*What pitcher had the highest percentage of walks (walks per inning pitched)? The lowest?*

Tommy Byrne, who pitched with the New York Yankees, St. Louis Browns and Washington Senators, was recognizable for his unique little move as he wound up to throw the ball: He would drop the ball from his gloved hand into his left hand as he came through with his delivery. But Byrne threw more than the ball; he threw many balls, leading the league in walks three times and in hit batsmen five times. In one year, 1949, he issued 179 walks in 196 innings pitched to establish the all-time season high for walks per inning pitched with a .913 average. The all-time low was the 0.68 of Babe Adams, who walked only 18 men in 263 innings pitched in 1920, to better the marks of Christy Mathewson, Cy Young and other control artists. The best and worst season walk percentages are:

### HIGHEST SEASON PERCENTAGE OF WALKS

| Year | Pitcher | BB | IP | % |
|------|---------|----|----|----|
| 1949 | Tommy Byrne | 179 | 196 | .913 |
| 1955 | Sam Jones | 185 | 242 | .764 |
| 1938 | Bob Feller | 208 | 278 | .748 |
| 1954 | Bob Turley | 181 | 247 | .732 |
| 1955 | Bob Turley | 177 | 247 | .716 |
| 1932 | Bump Hadley | 171 | 248 | .689 |
| 1974 | Nolan Ryan | 202 | 333 | .607 |
| 1937 | Bobo Newsom | 167 | 275 | .607 |
| 1915 | John Wycoff | 165 | 276 | .598 |
| 1938 | Bobo Newsom | 192 | 330 | .582 |

### LOWEST SEASON PERCENTAGE OF WALKS

| Year | Pitcher | BB | IP | % |
|------|---------|----|----|----|
| 1920 | Babe Adams | 18 | 264 | .068 |
| 1913 | Christy Mathewson | 21 | 306 | .069 |
| 1914 | Christy Mathewson | 23 | 312 | .074 |
| 1904 | Cy Young | 29 | 380 | .076 |
| 1933 | Red Lucas | 18 | 220 | .082 |
| 1919 | Babe Adams | 23 | 263 | .087 |
| 1919 | Slim Sallee | 20 | 228 | .087 |
| 1906 | Cy Young | 30 | 321 | .093 |
| 1902 | Deacon Phillippe | 26 | 272 | .096 |
| 1908 | Addie Joss | 30 | 325 | .092 |
| 1923 | Grover Alexander | 30 | 305 | .098 |

*What pitcher with more than ten at bats had the highest slugging average in World Series play?*

When the American League instituted the designated hitter rule in 1973, it was thought that American League pitchers hitting in World Series games would be penalized. But Oakland A's pitcher Ken Holtzman not only more than held his own as a hitting pitcher, he set World Series marks for a pitcher, with the highest slugging average for any pitcher with more than ten at bats in World Series play as well as tying for the lead in runs scored and setting the record for most doubles by a pitcher.

Holtzman's feat takes on even greater meaning when you consider that Babe Ruth had only one hit in 11 at bats while pitching in the Series for the Red Sox, and that Red Ruffing, another great-hitting pitcher, could collect only six hits in 34 trips to the plate. Here's a list of some of the more productive batters among World Series pitchers:

**WORLD SERIES PITCHERS
WITH HIGHEST SLUGGING AVERAGES**

| Pitcher | G | AB | R | H | 2B | 3B | HR | RBI | Bat. | Slug. |
|---|---|---|---|---|---|---|---|---|---|---|
| Jack Bentley | 10 | 12 | 1 | 5 | 1 | 0 | 1 | 2 | .417* | .750 |
| Dutch Ruether | 7 | 11 | 2 | 4 | 1 | 2* | 0 | 4 | .364 | .818 |
| Ken Holtzman | 8 | 12 | 4* | 4 | 3* | 0 | 1 | 1 | .333 | .833* |
| Jack Coombs | 6 | 24 | 1 | 8 | 1 | 0 | 0 | 4 | .333 | .375 |
| Dizzy Dean | 6 | 15 | 3 | 5 | 2 | 0 | 0 | 1 | .333 | .467 |
| Burleigh Grimes | 9 | 19 | 1 | 6 | 0 | 0 | 0 | 2 | .316 | .316 |
| Johnny Podres | 7 | 16 | 2 | 5 | 1 | 0 | 0 | 1 | .313 | .375 |
| Allie Reynolds | 15 | 26 | 2 | 8 | 1 | 0 | 0 | 2 | .308 | .346 |
| Ch. Mathewson | 11 | 32 | 2 | 9* | 0 | 0 | 0 | 1 | .281 | .281 |
| Red Ruffing | 14 | 34 | 1 | 6 | 1 | 0 | 0 | 4 | .176 | .206 |
| Bob Gibson | 9 | 28 | 4* | 4 | 0 | 0 | 2* | 3 | .143 | .357 |
| Dave McNally | 9 | 16 | 2 | 2 | 0 | 0 | 2* | 6* | .125 | .500 |
| Whitey Ford | 22* | 49* | 4* | 4 | 0 | 0 | 0 | 3 | .082 | .082 |

  * Leader in category

*Babe Ruth hit 69 home runs at the Polo Grounds as a member of the New York Yankees, and hit his first and last home runs there off the same pitcher. Name the pitcher.*

As a member of the New York Yankees in 1920, 1921 and 1922, Babe Ruth hit 69 homers at New York's Polo Grounds. His first one came on May 1, 1920, and was hit off Boston Red Sox left-hander Herb Pennock. His last home run as a member of the "home team" came on September 5, 1922, and again it was hit off Pennock. Ironically, Pennock joined the Yankees in 1923 and his 19 wins helped propel the Yankees to their third straight

American League pennant. In the World Series between the Yankees and the Giants, Ruth hit three towering home runs, all at the Polo Grounds and all in support of the same Herb Pennock, who won the only two games Ruth hit homers in.

*Who was the only pitcher to lead the league in sacrifice hits?*

Johnny Sain, of the Boston Braves, had 16 sacrifice hits in 1948 to lead the National League, the only pitcher to undisputedly lead his league in sacrifices.

*What two bespectacled pitchers had the most wins for one club in one year?*

Eyeglasses first appeared on the baseball scene in 1877, when a young pitcher for Boston in the National League named Will White wore them. This seeming disability didn't seem to reduce his effectiveness, as White went on to win 30 and 43 games the next two years.

But it was another 38 years before another bespectacled pitcher appeared in a major-league game—a pitcher called, appropriately enough, "Specs" Meadows. Lee Meadows came up with the St. Louis Cardinals in 1915 but was soon traded to the Pittsburgh Pirates, where he teamed up with another bespectacled pitcher, Carmen Hill (also called "Specs"), to win 41 games (19 for Meadows and 22 for Hill) and led the Pirates to the 1927 National League pennant, establishing a record for most wins for one club in one year by two bespectacled pitchers.

*What pitcher holds the record for most stolen bases?*

Bob Gibson stole 13 bases in his 17-year career, one more than Truett "Rip" Sewell, who stole 12 in his 13 years in the majors for the all-time base-stealing record for pitchers, and more than several regular ballplayers did in their lifetimes, such as Luke Easter, who stole only one base in 491 games, or Ernie Lombardi, who had eight steals in 1853 games.

> *What two Hall of Fame pitchers made their last major-league appearance against each other?*

Just as they met in battle many times before, including the memorable 1908 play-off game occasioned by Merkle's failure to touch second, Christy Mathewson and Mordecai Centennial "Three-Fingered" Brown hooked up in a duel on September 4, 1916, with Mathewson pitching his first game as pitcher-manager of the Cincinnati Reds and Brown pitching for the Cubs, a team he had returned to that year from the Federal League. It was to be the last time either future Hall of Famer ever appeared on a big-league mound, with Mathewson winning this one.

> *What was the most wins by a pitcher without a loss during a season?*

Tom Zachary's name is most prominently identified as the man who threw the 60th home run to Babe Ruth in the next-to-last game of the 1927 season. But the following year Zachary was sent by the Senators to join Ruth on the Yankees and started and won the third game of the 1928 Series as a surprise starter. In 1929 Zachary pitched in 26 games, 15 of them in relief, and posted a 12–0 record, the most wins by a pitcher without a loss during an entire season.

The National League record was set by Howie Krist of the 1941 St. Louis Cards, who pitched in 37 games, 29 of them in relief, and compiled a 10–0 record. Zachary's record was momentarily eclipsed, first by Johnny Allen of the Cleveland Indians, who in 1937 spun a string of 15 consecutive games, only to lose in his last game; and then by Elroy Face, who threw a "fork ball" in relief for the 1959 Pirates and won his first 18 games in relief, only to lose in his last appearance of the year, thereby establishing a record for the all-time high winning percentage, with .947.

*Who was the only pitcher to pitch no-hitters in each of his first two seasons in the majors?*

Only right-hander Steve Busby of the Kansas City Royals has thrown no-hitters in his first two years in the majors. Busby, who came up to Kansas City "for a cup of coffee" and five games in 1972, pitched in 37 games in his first full season with Kansas City in 1973, winning 16, including a no-hitter against the Detroit Tigers on April 27, 1973, and was selected as the American League Rookie Pitcher of the Year by *The Sporting News*. Busby came back to win 22 in his second full year, including a no-hitter against Milwaukee on June 19, 1974, thereby becoming the only pitcher to throw no-hitters in his first two years in the major leagues.

*Who was the first black pitcher in the majors?*

Brooklyn's Dan Bankhead, who appeared in his first major-league game on August 8, 1947, and celebrated it by hitting a home run in his first time at bat in the majors— his only homer in the majors—was the first black pitcher in the major leagues. Bankhead pitched in just 52 games, winning nine and losing five, before dropping out of baseball in 1951.

*Who was the last pitcher to legally throw a spitball?*

When Burleigh Grimes retired at the end of the 1934 season, he was the last of the 18 pitchers who had been allowed to continue throwing a "legal" spitball by the joint Rules Committee of the American and National Leagues, which banned the pitch, along with the "shineball" and "other freak pitches," for the 1920 season.

Originally developed by Elmer Stricklett, a relatively obscure pitcher with the Brooklyn Dodgers from 1905 to 1907, the "spitball" provided many pitchers with a pitch that broke peculiarly. Of those 18 active pitchers allowed to use the spitball "until the ends of their careers," two retired in 1920, two more in 1921, and only four reached the Thirties—Red Faber, Clarence Mitchell, Jack Quinn and Grimes. Grimes loaded the spitball with the saliva stimulated by his wad of gum; and in the beginning of his career, many of the opposing batters could read whether a spitter was coming by how he chewed his gum. But by the twilight of his 19-year career, Grimes had mastered the pitch and wound up with 270 wins and four 20-game seasons.

In later years many pitchers were accused of "doctoring" the ball with illegal saliva to give it its peculiar breaking properties. But only Preacher Roe admitted he threw one—in an article in the *Saturday Evening Post* the month after he left baseball. In 1942 Bobo Newsom was caught throwing a spitter by manager Leo Durocher of the Dodgers, who suspended him for throwing it and "lying to me about it." But perhaps the best commentary on the continued use of the spitter came from American League umpire Hank Soar. Reacting one day to the constant protests of the opposing team to the deliveries by Boston Red Sox pitchers, Soar asked to inspect the ball and found it to be wiped immaculately clean. In exasperation, he spat on it himself and returned it to the pitcher.

The list of active spitballers who were allowed to continue their unique delivery "until the ends of their careers" follows:

## LAST LEGAL SPITBALLERS

| National League | American League |
|---|---|
| Bill Doak (1912–29) | Yancey "Doc" Ayers (1913–21) |
| Phil Douglas (1912–22) | Ray Caldwell (1910–21) |
| Dana Fillingim (1915–25) | Stan Coveleski (1912–28) |
| Ray Fisher (1910–20) | Urban Faber (1914–33) |
| Marvin Goodwin (1916–25) | Hub Leonard (1913–25)* |
| Burleigh Grimes (1916–34) | Jack Quinn (1909–33) |
| Claude Hendrix (1911–20) | Allan Russell (1915–25) |
| Clarence Mitchell (1911–32)* | Urban Shocker (1916–28) |
| Dick Rudolph (1910–27) | Allan Sothoron (1914–26) |
| * Left-hander | |

*When Bob Feller struck out a record 348 batters in 1946, who was the only American League regular that he didn't strike out?*

Feller struck out every player who played regularly during the 1946 season except outfielder Barney McCosky of the Philadelphia A's and Detroit Tigers. McCosky, traded during the year to the A's for third baseman George Kell, appeared in 127 games and came to bat 399 times with just 22 strikeouts, none against Feller in his record-setting year.

*Who served up the most home-run balls to Hank Aaron?*

Hank Aaron's favorite pitcher was Don Drysdale of the Brooklyn and Los Angeles Dodgers, who was victimized no less than 17 times by Aaron in the 14 years he pitched against him. Aaron's next-favorite victim was Claude Osteen, also of the Los Angeles Dodgers, along with the Cincinnati Reds, Houston Astros and St. Louis Cardinals, whom Aaron outguessed on 13 homers. And, of course, another Dodger, Al Downing, gave up just two—numbers 676 and 715—but will always be associated with Aaron's home-run records.

*Who were the other pitchers on the 1948 Boston Braves' staff?*

The little ditty that went "Spahn and Sain and two days' rain" is as ingrained a part of baseball legend as the "Tinker-to-Evers-to-Chance" phrase that had captured the imagination of baseball some 40 years before. But just as Harry Steinfeldt had been the missing name in the "Tinker-to-Evers-to-Chance" verse, so were names like Bill Voiselle and Vern Bickford, who fleshed out the Spahn and Sain starting rotation.

In fact, the tandem of Spahn and Sain won only 39 games out of the 91 the 1948 Braves won on their way to the pennant, a total that falls far short of the 49 won by Paul and Dizzy Dean for the 1934 Cardinals, the 52 won by Bucky Walters and Paul Derringer for the 1939 Reds or the 67 won by Christy Mathewson and Joe McGinnity for the 1904 Giants, all National League pennant winners. And had it not been for Voiselle's 13 wins, Bickford's 11 wins, Red Barrett's seven wins, Clyde Shoun's five wins and Bobby Hogue's eight wins, the Braves would not have been able to finish ahead of the Cardinals and the Dodgers, regardless of how much rain fell on Boston.

*What American League pitcher allowed the most runs in one inning?*

On July 7, 1923, left-hander Frank O'Doul took the mound in the sixth inning for the Boston Red Sox to face the Cleveland Indians. O'Doul, who had won 25 games for San Francisco in 1921 and had been a throw-in in the trade that brought Joe Dugan to the Yankees just one year earlier, was used as a reliever for an incredibly weak pitching staff for the last-place Red Sox, consisting of Howard Ehmke, "Old" Jack Quinn and some has-beens who never were. In what was to become known as "The Indian Massacre," O'Doul faced 16 Cleveland batters and gave up 13 runs in Boston's 27–3 loss, a negative American League record that still stands—and ended whatever dreams he ever had about becoming a big-league pitcher.

The last-place Red Sox, who desperately could have used pitching help from anyone, soon sent O'Doul down to Salt Lake City, where he pitched in just 24 games the following year and tried his hand in the outfield. The experiment proved successful; O'Doul batted .392 in 116 games, tying for the Pacific Coast League lead and starting a second career as a hitting outfielder, which brought him back up to the National League. There "Lefty" O'Doul led the league in batting twice and set the National league record for most hits in a season with 254.

*Name the two pitchers who allowed the fewest hits in a double shutout.*

When Paul Dean pitched a no-hitter against the Brooklyn Dodgers in the second game of a doubleheader on September 21, 1934, his brother "Dizzy" said, "Shucks, if I'da known he was going to do that, I'da pitched a no-hitter, too."

In fact, Jerome Hannah "Dizzy" Dean had come close to that in the first game, allowing the Dodgers just three singles and no runs, thereby giving the Deans the honor of being the pitching teammates who allowed the fewest number of hits in one double shutout.

*Who was the youngest pitcher to win 300 games?*

There have been 14 300-game winners, many winning their 300th game after they turned 40. The pitcher who won 300 at the earliest age was a kid compared to most of the other late-starting pitchers who achieved this magic total—so, naturally enough, he was called "Kid." Charles Augustus "Kid" Nichols, who had won 294 games before he turned 30, won his 300th game on July 7, 1900, at the age of 30 and in his 11th year in the majors. Nichols, who had ten straight seasons of 20 or more wins, including seven 30-game seasons, pitched for just four more years and won just 62 more games, to give him a total of 362 wins.

*What two pitchers were taken out in the eighth inning while pitching no-hitters?*

Clay Kirby, pitching for the San Diego Padres against the New York Mets on July 21, 1970, had a no-hitter after eight innings. But in the bottom of the eighth, manager Preston Gomez pulled Kirby for a pinch hitter, and the Mets got a hit in the ninth to win the game and break up the no-hitter.

Four years later Don Wilson, the Houston Astro pitcher, found himself in much the same situation. Pitching no-hit ball against the Cincinnati Reds on September 4, 1974, Wilson was lifted for a pinch hitter in the bottom of the eighth, and the Reds broke up the no-hitter in the ninth. The manager of the Houston Astros at the time was the same Preston Gomez, who was consistent, if not correct, in his strategy.

*Name the two pitchers who gave up homers to Ruth in his 60-home-run season and hits to DiMaggio in his 56-game streak.*

Thirty-four pitchers gave up home runs to Babe Ruth for his record-setting 60 homers in 1927. Forty-three different pitchers gave up hits to Joe DiMaggio in his record-setting 56-game streak in 1941. Among them, two pitchers gave up homers to Ruth *and* hits to DiMaggio—Ted Lyons and Lefty Grove, both members of the Hall of Fame. Lyons, who came up to the White Sox directly from Baylor University in 1923, threw home run number 54 to Ruth at Yankee Stadium on September 18, 1927, and gave up two singles to DiMaggio on July 13, 1941, to keep his streak alive at 52 consecutive games. Grove, who came up to the Philadelphia A's in 1925, gave up home run number 57 to Ruth at Yankee Stadium on September 27 and, in his last full year as a member of the Boston Red Sox staff, gave up a single to DiMaggio on May 25, 1941.

*Who was the only man to pitch to both Babe Ruth and Mickey Mantle?*

The only pitcher to face both Ruth and Mantle was Al Benton, who pitched in the American League for the A's, Tigers, Indians and Red Sox from 1934 to 1952, with five years spent in the minors and in military service. Benton pitched against Ruth while with the Philadelphia A's and against Mantle while toiling for the Red Sox.

The only other pitcher who spanned the careers of both Yankee sluggers was Louis Norman "Bobo" Newsom, who pitched for several clubs in both leagues from 1929 through 1953. However, Newsom didn't pitch in the American League until 1934, Ruth's last year, when he did face Ruth. But the year Mantle came up, 1951, Newsom was out of the majors. He came back to pitch in 1952 and 1953 with the Philadelphia A's (again) and the Washington Senators (again). In his 24 appearances in 1952 he didn't face the Yankees, and in his only mound appearance against the Yankees in 1953, on August 15, Mantle was injured and not in the lineup.

*What son of a famous major-league pitcher broke up Joe DiMaggio's longest consecutive-hitting streak?*

On the night of July 17, 1941, Joe DiMaggio went to bat four times in an attempt to preserve his 56-consecutive-game hitting streak. He faced Cleveland's starting pitcher, Al Smith, three times and hit two sizzling drives down the third-base line only to be robbed by Indian third baseman Ken Keltner and walked once. In his last appearance at the plate Jim Bagby, Jr., a young right-hander and son of the famous Cleveland Indian pitcher Jim Bagby, Sr., retired DiMaggio on a shot that shortstop Lou Boudreau converted into a double play. DiMaggio went on afterward to hit in 17 more consecutive games, and counting the 1941 All-Star game on July 8, hit in 75 of 76 consecutive games.

This was *not* Joe DiMaggio's longest consecutive-hit skein! In his second year in professional ball, as a member of the San Francisco Seals, DiMaggio had hit in 61 consecutive games, amassing 104 hits in 257 official times at bat. On July 25, 1933, the 18-year-old sensation faced Oakland pitcher Ed Walsh, Jr., son of Chicago White Sox Hall of Famer Ed Walsh, Sr., who held him hitless in five times at bat.

But even DiMaggio's 61-game streak was not the longest in organized ball. Former major-leaguer Joe Wilhoit of Wichita in the Western League had hit in 67 consecutive games back in 1919 and earned an immediate return to the Boston Red Sox outfield, where he played alongside Babe Ruth for all of five games to end his career.

*Name the only pitcher to win 200 games and never have a 20-game season.*

Of the more than 170 pitchers who have won 200 or more games, only one pitcher accomplished this feat without having a single 20-game season—Milt Pappas. Pappas won 209 games in his 17-year career, never won more than 17 games in any one season and is the only member of this relatively exclusive club to have 200 lifetime wins without at least one 20-game season.

*Name the only team to have four knuckleballers.*

The 1944 Washington Senators' pitching staff included four knuckle-ball pitchers—Dutch Leonard, Johnny Niggling, Roger Wolff and Mickey Haefner—together with Early Wynn, but could manage only 64 wins among them, finishing in eighth place, seven full games behind the seventh-place White Sox. But the next year, their last together as a quartet, these same four managed to propel the Senators into second place, only one and a half games behind the pennant-winning Tigers, with Wolff winning 20 games, third highest in the league.

*What pitcher had the highest lifetime batting average?*

George Uhle, who pitched 17 years with Detroit and Cleveland, had a .288 lifetime batting average, the highest lifetime batting average of any pitcher. Ranking behind Uhle were Red Lucas, who hit .281 in 16 years with the Giants, Braves, Reds and Pirates; Wes Ferrell, who had a .280 average in 15 years playing primarily with the Indians and Red Sox; Don Newcombe, who compiled a .271 average in ten years with the Dodgers, Reds and Indians; and Red Ruffing's .269 average in 22 years with the Red Sox, Yankees and White Sox. The best single-season average for a pitcher was Walter Johnson's .433 in 1925 when, at the age of 37, the "Big Train" had 42 hits in 97 times at bat to unofficially lead the league in hitting and his team to the American League pennant, throwing into the bargain his last 20-game season.

*Name the only two father-and-son pitching combinations in which both have won over 50 games.*

Of the 14 father-son pitching combinations since 1900, only the Bagbys and the Colemans have posted 50 wins apiece. Jim Bagby, Sr., pitching for Cincinnati, Cleveland and Pittsburgh, won 128 games, while Jim Bagby, Jr., won 97, spending time with the Red Sox, Indians and Pirates. Joseph Patrick "Joe" Coleman had a 52-76 won-lost mark for the A's, Orioles and Tigers, while his son, Joseph Howard "Joe" Coleman, won over 100 games pitching for Washington and Detroit.

> *Who was the youngest pitcher ever to win 30 games in a season?*

Twenty-one pitchers have won 30 or more games in a season, with Christy Mathewson winning 30 four times, Alexander three times and Johnson, Young and McGinnity twice. But the youngest pitcher ever to win 30 games only passed the milestone once and he did it when he was but 22 years old. "Smokey" Joe Wood, pitching for the Boston Red Sox in 1912 with the new cork-center ball which had replaced the pitcher's friend, the dead ball, pitched ten shutouts, won 16 straight games and had an ERA of 1.91 in putting together a record of 34 wins and only five losses. He went on to win three games in the 1912 World Series, becoming one of only a handful of pitchers who have won three games in a Series.

Wood, who had had a 1.68 ERA at the age of 20 and had won 79 games by the time he turned 23—more than any other modern pitcher—suffered a broken hand in 1913 and only won nine games. He came back to win 15 after another nine-game season, but then a sore shoulder and a holdout ended his career and he never won another game in the majors after 1915. But Joe Wood turned to the outfield and played five more years for the Cleveland Indians, batting .298 and ending his career as only one of four players who ever had over 100 wins and over 500 hits.

> *Who was the only pitcher to hit two home runs in a game in which he pitched a no-hitter?*

Many pitchers have hit home runs—most notably Jim Tobin, who hit three in one game; Wes Ferrell, who had 38 lifetime homers; and Red Ruffing, who had 36 lifetime homers—and many more have pitched no-hitters. But the only time a pitcher hit two home runs during a game in which he was also pitching a no-hitter was on June 23, 1971, when Rick Wise of the Phillies no-hit the Cincinnati Reds 4–0 and hit two home runs to drive in more runs than he needed.

*What pitcher won the greatest percentage of his team's victories in one year?*

Steve Carlton, pitching for the last-place Philadelphia Phillies of 1972, won 27 of the team's 59 victories, 45.8 percent of the team's total victories. Other pitchers who carried more than their share of the burden of their team's total victories include "Noodles" Hahn, who won 42.3 percent of the 1901 Cincinnati Reds' total victories (22 of 52 wins); Joe Bush, who won 41.7 percent of the 1916 A's' total wins (15 of 36 victories); Eddie Rommel, who won 41.5 percent of the 1922 A's' total wins (27 of 65 wins); and Walter Johnson, who won 40 percent of the 1912 Washington Senators' total victories (36 of 90 wins).

*What two pitchers had the best won-lost records against the Yankees?*

The two most effective pitchers against the Yankees were two left-handers: Dickie Kerr, who pitched for the White Sox for four years and had a 14-4 record against the Yankees for a .778 average; and George Herman "Babe" Ruth, who pitched for the Red Sox for four full seasons and part of two others and won 17 and lost only five against the Yankees for a .773 average.

*What pitcher struck out every time he came to bat one year?*

In 1955, his first year in the majors, Brooklyn's Sandy Koufax came up to bat 12 times and struck out 12 times, a perfect record in futility. And Koufax's 12 strikeouts in his rookie season marked the lowest total number of times he struck out in a season. He struck out almost once out of every two times up during his 12-year career.

*Name the only two pitchers to win at least 100 games in each league.*

Only two pitchers—Cy Young and Jim Bunning—have won at least 100 games in each league. Young, baseball's all-time winningest pitcher, won 290 games in the National League and 221 in the American League, the only man to win 200 games in each league! Jim Bunning won 118 games in the American League and 106 in the National, also throwing no-hitters, as Young had before him, in each league. Milt Pappas, who just missed pitching a perfect game against the Padres on September 2, 1972, when he walked the 27th man to face him after retiring the first 26 and then got the final out on a routine pop fly, also just missed joining Bunning and Young in the "100-in-each-league" club. Pappas won 110 games in the American League and 99 in the National.

*What left-handed Hall of Famer had the most victories by the time he turned 23?*

Forty-one pitchers are enshrined in the Hall of Fame at Cooperstown, and only ten of them are left-handers. But the left-hander who had won more games before he was 23 was none of the ten elected as pitchers. It was George Herman "Babe" Ruth, who had amassed a total of 67 wins and only 34 losses for a .663 winning percentage by the time his 23rd birthday rolled around on February 6, 1918. Ruth's credentials as a pitcher are comparable to any of the other ten: He is the only man to win an ERA title and a home-run championship as well; he was the winner in the longest game ever played in World Series history, going the distance to win a 2–1 decision in 14 innings in 1916, starting his then record of 27⅔ scoreless innings in World Series competition; and he possesses the second best won-lost percentage ever compiled against the Yankees.

*Who was the runner who got on base in Ernie Shore's "perfect game"?*

When Ray Morgan, the Washington second baseman, led off the Washington-Boston game on June 23, 1917, by getting a base on balls on a disputed pitch, Red Sox pitcher Babe Ruth stormed home-plate umpire Clarence Owens. Ruth first argued with Owens, then screamed at him and finally struck him behind the ear after he was ejected from the game. Ernie Shore was brought in by Red Sox manager Jack Barry to relieve the expelled Ruth. Moments later the speedy Morgan was thrown out attempting to steal, by Boston catcher Sam Agnew, and Shore went on to retire the final 26 men in order, getting credit for his own "perfect game," the "shortest" perfect game in baseball history.

*Who pitched the longest no-hitter in the history of organized baseball?*

In 1909, his first year in pro baseball, Fred Toney pitched a 17-inning no-hitter for the Winchester, Kentucky, club in the Blue Grass (Class D) League. Toney, who was to gain immortality just eight years later as the winning pitcher in baseball's only double no-hit game, pitched inning after inning and found that his teammates could be sued for nonsupport, but not the town of Winchester. For as goose eggs were hung up on the scoreboard, the news of Toney's achievement spread throughout the eastern Kentucky town, and church bells rang, fire engines clanged and the townsfolk mobbed the park to catch a glimpse of some history in the making. Finally, in the bottom of the 17th, Winchester scored and Fred Toney won the longest no-hitter in the history of organized baseball.

*Name the two pitchers who pitched for 22 consecutive seasons in the major leagues.*

Only seven pitchers have pitched over 20 years, and only two pitched for 22 consecutive years—Sad Sam Jones and Cy Young. Early Wynn, Red Ruffing and Herb Pennock all pitched 22 years (and Wynn part of a 23rd, in search of his 300th win), but all of them had their careers interrupted by military service and thus did not pitch for 22 consecutive seasons in the majors.

# 4TH INNING

## THE FIELDERS

*How many double plays did the Tinker-Evers-Chance combination make in four World Series?*

The threesome of Tinker-Evers-Chance played in the 1906, 1907, 1908 and 1910 World Series and pulled off just one double play in the 21 games in those four Series. In 1907 Frank Chance was hit by a pitch thrown by "Wild" Bill Donovan and didn't play in the fifth and last game of that Series. In 1910 Johnny Evers was injured and didn't play in that five-game Series. So the combination of Tinker-Evers-Chance only played in 15 World Series games together.

In those 15 games, the Cubs made 13 double plays: four on line drives, two on flies in which the runner was doubled up, one on a strikeout and caught-stealing play, and six on ground balls to the infield. Of those six to the infield, one went from Steinfeldt to Evers to Chance, one went from "Three-Fingered" Brown to Tinker to Chance, one went from Evers, unassisted, to Chance, two went from Tinker, unassisted, to Chance, and one went from Tinker to Evers to Chance. But even this double play, which would fuel the reputation of this "great" double-play combination, is reported in the record books as a Tinker, unassisted, to Chance double play. One has to go to the box score for the October 10, 1907, game against the Tigers to see that the play on a ground ball by Cobb went from Tinker to Evers to Chance. (And, to reconstruct the play, it would be unthinkable for Tinker to be overshifted against Cobb, one of the great scientific batters of all time, giving him a gaping hole at shortstop in which to slap a hit, but would be playing in his normal shortstop position, setting up the only Tinker-to-Evers-to-Chance double play in World Series history.)

*Which catcher allowed the most runners to steal bases in one game?*

On the afternoon of June 28, 1907, Wesley Branch Rickey, catcher for the New York Highlanders, suffered through the most humiliating day any catcher ever experienced. No less than 13 Washington Senators stole bases on him, an all-time record for catcher futility. Rickey, who was to catch only a few more games in the majors and leave the active playing ranks at the end of the season, saw the Senators steal as many bases in that one game as they did in the entire 1957 season.

*Name the only three brothers to start a regular-season game together as the three outfielders.*

On September 22, 1963, the three Alou brothers—Felipe, Matty and Jesus—comprised the starting outfield for the San Francisco Giants against the New York Mets at the Polo Grounds, the only time three brothers have appeared in an outfield at the same time for a major-league club. The St. Louis Cardinals started the three Cruz brothers—Hector, Jose and Tommy—in one outfield during an exhibition game in Florida in 1973, but the Alous stand alone as the only brother act to start in the outfield during the regular season.

Only one other time has a family act so dominated a lineup. It came when the St. Louis Cardinals, in the late '40s, started an all-Schoendienst infield during one of their spring training games. But spring training, as so many clubs and rookie "phenoms" find out, is not the big leagues—a rule that also applies to triviots and their questions.

*Who was the only nonpitcher to win a Golden Glove award in both leagues?*

Outfielder Tommie Agee won the Golden Glove, a symbolic award made to the best fielders at their respective positions, while with the Chicago White Sox in 1965 and with the New York Mets in 1970, the year after he had made two of the most heralded catches in World Series history, to lead the Mets to a win over the favored Orioles.

## Who was the last left-handed catcher?

There have been ten left-handed catchers in baseball history, but only three played in modern baseball, and only one—Dale Long, who caught two games for the 1958 Chicago Cubs—in recent times. The seven who caught before the turn of the century are: Bill Harbidge, who caught 125 games from 1876 through 1884; Fergy Malone of the 1876 Philadelphia Nationals, who caught 21 games over two seasons; Cal Broughton, who caught 35 games for six teams between 1883 and 1888; Phil Baker, who caught 62 games from 1883 through 1886; John Humphries, who caught 75 games in 1883 and 1884; Pop Tate, who caught 202 games from 1885 through 1890; and Jack Clements, the premiere left-handed catcher of all time, who caught 1073 games—more than Roger Bresnahan—primarily for the Philadelphia Phillies from 1884 through 1900. The only two other than Long to catch in a major-league game in the twentieth century were Joe Wall, who caught seven games for the Giants and Dodgers in 1901 and 1902, and Tom Doran, who caught 46 games for the Red Sox and Tigers from 1904 through 1906.

The combined batting average for these ten left-handed catchers was .261, not bad for catchers—right- or left-handed (especially when you consider that the combined lifetime batting average for ten right-handed catchers—Yogi Berra, Roy Campanella, Gabby Hartnett, Roger Bresnahan, George Gibson, Jim Hegan, Ray Schalk, Bill Carrigan, Bill Killefer and Billy Sullivan— all considered greats or near greats, was *also* .261).

### Who caught the most no-hitters?

Ray Schalk of the Chicago White Sox caught four no-hitters in his 17-year career as a major-league backstop. Schalk, elected to the Hall of Fame in 1955, caught James Scott's no-hitter in 1914, Joseph Benz's in 1914, Eddie Cicotte's in 1917 and Charlie Robertson's perfect game in 1922.

Ten other catchers have been on the receiving end of baseball history three times: Lou Criger (1904, 1908 and 1910); Bill Carrigan (1911, 1916 and 1916); Val Picinich (1916, 1920 and 1923); Luke Sewell (1931, 1935 and 1937); Jim Hegan (1947, 1948 and 1951); Yogi Berra (1951, 1951 and 1956); Roy Campanella (1952, 1956 and 1956); Del Crandall (1954, 1960 and 1960); Johnny Edwards (1965, 1965 and 1968); and Jeff Torborg (1965, 1970 and 1973).

Picinich is the only catcher to catch no-hitters with three different teams, handling Joe Bush's no-hitter for the A's in 1916, Walter Johnson's masterpiece for the Senators in 1920 and Howard Ehmke's with the Red Sox in 1923. Jeff Torborg, along with Gus Triandos, caught no-hitters in both leagues: Sandy Koufax's fourth no-hitter while with the Dodgers and Nolan Ryan's first no-hitter with the Angels. (Triandos caught Hoyt Wilhelm's 1958 no-hitter for the Orioles and Jim Bunning's perfect game for the Phillies in 1964.)

### Which of the three DiMaggio brothers had the highest fielding average?

Although Dom and Joe are remembered as great center fielders, it was older brother Vince who had the higher lifetime fielding average. Vince, also a center

fielder, was best remembered for leading the National
League in strikeouts for six of his ten years as a player. Yet he led the National League in assists for three
seasons and in putouts for two, and had a .981 fielding
average to the .978 of his younger brothers.

*Who was the first outfielder to wear sunglasses?*

Harry Hooper, the brilliant right fielder in the Duffy
Lewis—Tris Speaker—Harry Hooper outfield that led
the Boston Red Sox to four World Championships in
nine years, purchased a pair of sunglasses from a leading optometrist to shade his eyes from the sun's wicked
glare in Fenway Park's right-field area, becoming the
first outfielder to wear sunglasses.

*Who was the only first baseman to have three
assists in one inning?*

Everybody remembers "Dr. Strangeglove," better
known as Dick Stuart, whose nickname came from his
ineptness with his glove. But it was his bat that sup-
plied his ticket to the major leagues. Brought up by
the Pirates after hitting 66 home runs for the Lincoln,
Nebraska, team in the Class A Western League in
1956, Stuart became one of only four men to hit 30
or more home runs in each league, hitting a high of
35 for the Pirates in 1961 and 42 for the Red Sox in
1963.

However, no number of homers could take the fans'
minds off his fielding—Stuart held the major-league
mark for most times leading the league in errors at
first, leading or tying in seven of his nine years in the
majors. But one year—1963—he led the American
League first basemen in putouts and assists, and on
the afternoon of June 28 he set an all-time record by

assisting in all three of the first-inning outs. A strange feat for "Dr. Strangeglove."

*Who holds the record for most chances accepted by a first baseman in a doubleheader in both leagues?*

Hal Chase was generally acknowledged to be the greatest-fielding first baseman of all time. Clark Griffith referred to Hal as the most graceful player he had ever seen, while Grantland Rice listed him on his all-time team of "Smart Players." He was the first to play off first so that he could cover more territory than first basemen had been used to doing until he arrived on the scene, fresh from Santa Clara University, where he played under Joe Corbett, brother of the former heavyweight champ. Jumping teams, leagues and baseball itself occasionally, Chase played for five major-league teams, several semipro teams and three major leagues—the American, the National and the Federal.

While Chase's far-ranging play caused him some difficulties—he led the league in errors six times—he was able to get to the ball more often than most first basemen. In 1905, his very first year in professional baseball, as the first baseman with the New York Highlanders, Chase handled 38 chances, setting the major-league record. And in his very last year in professional baseball, 1919, he set the National League record, handling 35 chances in a doubleheader for the New York Giants.

*Against what home-run slugger was the "Williams Shift" first used?*

The "Williams Shift" was first employed back in the late Twenties by the Chicago Cubs against that great home-run hitter Fred "Cy" Williams of the Philadelphia Phillies. Although Cleveland Indian manager Lou Boudreau is given credit for "inventing" the "Williams Shift" to defend against Ted Williams, this exaggerated overshift of the infield was actually devised some 30 years earlier to protect against Cy Williams.

Interestingly, Ted and Cy Williams have more in common than merely being the reasons for an overshifted infeld: They were both left-handed sluggers; both led their respective leagues in home runs four times and home-run percentage five times; both were feared pull hitters, able to drive ball after ball into the right-field area, but relatively ineffectual going to left field; and both disdained using the bunt toward the empty third-base area, choosing instead to challenge the "Shift" and drive the ball through to right field, which they both did with a reasonable degree of success.

> Who is the only major-league center fielder ever to have caught a foul ball?

Many swift-footed center fielders have had to cover for slow-of-foot right and left fielders whose presence in the lineup was dictated only by their ability with the bat. One exceptional speed merchant was Johnny Mostil, who played center field for the Chicago White Sox in the Twenties. Mostil led the American League in steals twice, in runs once, in putouts twice, total chances per game three times and fielding average once. His left fielder was Bibb Falk, who on this bright, sunny spring day was somewhat unconcerned with a high looping foul in Nashville's Sulphur Dell ball park. Mostil, sensing that Falk had given up on catching it, sprinted past the foul line and lunged into the stands after the ball, coming up with the only putout on a foul ball ever registered by a center fielder.

There have been other center fielders who were said

to cover the foul lines. One was Frankie Baumholtz, who played center field for the Chicago Cubs between Ralph Kiner and Hank Sauer, hardly merchants of speed, for one long year and a half—a year and a half that must have aged him ten and cut short both his baseball and basketball careers. After hearing Kiner and Sauer shouting to Baumholtz "You got it, Frankie" and "Lots of room, Frankie" time after time, a Chicago sportswriter dubbed Baumholtz "the bravest center fielder of all time." Nevertheless, it was Johnny Mostil not Baumholtz who caught the only foul ball ever caught by a center fielder.

### What outfielder participated in two triple plays in one season?

Charlie Jamieson, Cleveland outfielder, participated in two triple plays in 1928, against the White Sox on May 23 and against the Yankees just four weeks later, on June 19. Paul Hines, center fielder for the Providence team in the National League in 1878, was credited with putting three men out on one ball, and was credited with the first unassisted triple play in major-league history, although eyewitness reports dispute the fact that it was unassisted. But Walter Carlisle, playing in the outfield for the Vernon, California, team in the Pacific Coast League, turned in an unassisted triple play against Los Angeles on August 19, 1911, the only authenticated unassisted triple play by an outfielder in the history of organized baseball.

### Who was the only player to both pitch and catch in both leagues?

Many players have both pitched and caught in the majors, including Cesar Tovar and Bert Campaneris (both of whom played every one of the nine positions on a team in the course of one nine-inning game), George Uhle, Fred Mitchell, Chris Short, Jimmie Foxx,

Roger Bresnahan, Cal McVey and Cap Anson. But only one man has ever pitched and caught in both leagues. Mike Ryba, who came up to the Cardinals in 1935 at the age of 32, caught seven games for them in four years while appearing 57 times on the mound, and caught three games in six years with the Boston Red Sox, appearing 183 times as a pitcher. On one occasion, Ryba pitched the first game of a double-header and caught the second.

*Who played center field for the Cleveland Indians the day Bob Feller threw a no-hitter against the Yankees?*

Someone once asked Cleveland Indian pitcher Bob Lemon if he preferred to pitch and he said, "No, give me the outfield. I want to be in there playing every day." And Lemon, who played 14 games in the outfield for the Cleveland Indians in 1946 and 1947, was playing center field in Yankee Stadium on April 30, 1946, when Bob Feller pitched a no-hitter against the Yankees.

*Who was the only man to hit a home run in the same game in which he pulled an unassisted triple play?*

There have been eight unassisted triple plays, seven in regular season play and one in World Series competition, dating back to the first one, executed by Cleveland shortstop Neal Ball on July 19, 1909, down to Washington shortstop Ron Hansen on July 30, 1968. But Neal Ball was the only one of the eight who hit a home run in the same game, hitting his homer in the bottom of the second after pulling his unassisted triple play in the top half of the inning. This celebrated drive was the only homer Ball hit during the entire season and only one of four he hit in over 1600 at bats during his career.

## 5TH INNING

# THE WORLD SERIES

*Who was the winning pitcher in the World Series
game won by Cookie Lavagetto's double?*

When Harry "Cookie" Lavagetto delivered his last big-
league hit, a two-out, one-strike double over Yankee right
fielder Tommy Henrich's head to score Eddie Miksis and
Al Gionfriddo and give the Brooklyn Dodgers a 3–2 win
over the Yankees in the fourth game of the 1947 World
Series, he lost the game and a no-hitter for Floyd "Bill"
Bevans. But if Bevans lost the game and his no-hitter, he
gained instant immortality for his effort—he was just one
out away from pitching the first no-hitter in World Series
history.

Also lost was the name of the winning pitcher, Brooklyn
relief ace Hugh Casey, who had come on in the top of the
ninth and, with the bases loaded and one out, had retired
the side on just one pitch. His one pitch was to his old
nemesis, Tommy Henrich, who had been at bat six years
before when Casey threw a pitch that got away from
Brooklyn catcher Mickey Owen after Henrich had apparently struck out to end the game, and opened the floodgates
for the Yankees in the fourth game of the '41 Series.

But this time when Casey threw the same pitch, a "wet"
curve, Henrich slapped the ball back to him. Casey threw
home to force the runner, and catcher Bruce Edwards's
throw to first doubled up Henrich, ending the inning.
Lavagetto's blow in the bottom of the ninth also made
Casey a winner for the second time in two days, the first
time in Series history that a pitcher won two games in two
days (a feat later equaled by Cincinnati's Ross Grimsley
in the 1972 Series).

Other winners who have been overlooked in the loser's
"immortality" are Larry Jansen, the winning pitcher in the
1951 play-off game between the Dodgers and the Giants
won by Bobby Thomson's three-run homer off Ralph
Branca; Lew Burdette, the winning pitcher when Harvey
Haddix lost his 12-inning perfect game in 1959; and Ray

Kremer, the Pittsburgh reliever who won the rain-soaked seventh game of the '25 Series lost by Walter Johnson.

> *When Enos Slaughter scored from first on a single to win the seventh and deciding game of the 1946 World Series, who hit the single? Who was the center fielder who retrieved it? Who was the shortstop who took the throw and relayed it to the plate? Who was the catcher who got the ball too late? And who were the winning and losing pitchers?*

With the score 3–3 in the bottom of the eighth in the final and deciding contest of the 1946 World Series between the St. Louis Cardinals and the Boston Red Sox, one man took it upon himself to break the deadlock, and did—with many handmaidens to history aiding his one-man show.

The Red Sox had tied the game 3–3 with two runs in the top of the eighth, but center fielder Dom DiMaggio had twisted his ankle coming into second with the hit that had tied up the game. He was replaced in the bottom of the eighth by Leon Culberson in center, and Boston manager Joe Cronin also brought in a new pitcher, Bob Klinger, to hold the Cardinals.

The first man to face Klinger was Enos "Country" Slaughter, who promptly singled for the Cards' eighth hit. After Whitey Kurowski and Del Rice were retired, Harry "The Hat" Walker came up with a hit-and-run signal on. Walker drove the ball into center, and Slaughter, running with the pitch, rounded second and headed for third as Culberson, slightly slower than DiMaggio, chased the ball down. Then, despite third-base coach Mike Gonzalez's outstretched hands signaling for him to hold up at third, Slaughter continued tearing around the bases and headed for home.

Boston shortstop Johnny Pesky, seeing Gonzalez's signal and fully expecting Slaughter to stop at third, took the relay from Culberson and held it for a split second before turning around. Only then did Pesky grasp the situation and fire the ball home to Boston catcher Roy Partee, who had taken over for Hal Wagner behind the plate. But too late. Slaughter slid in around Partee's tag and made the Cardinals the World Champions for the sixth time and Harry "The Cat" Brecheen the winner in relief. It was Brecheen's third win in the Series, making him the first left-hander ever to win three games in one Series (a mark tied 22 years later by Mickey Lolich when he beat the Cards three times for the Tigers—all in complete games).

*Who was the only Dodger to get as many as three balls off Don Larsen in his perfect game?*

Only Pee Wee Reese, Brooklyn Dodgers shortstop, got as many as three balls off the offerings of Don Larsen in the fifth game of the 1956 World Series, as the Yankee hurler pitched the most famous "no hits, no runs, no nothing" game in baseball history. Larsen, of whom former manager Jimmy Dykes had said, "The only thing Don Larsen fears is sleep," was a footloose pitcher who had been best remembered previous to his perfect game on October 8, 1956, for his 3-21 record with the Baltimore Orioles in 1954. Traded to the Yankees with Bob Turley, Larsen began to emerge as a winning pitcher, posting an 11-5 record for the American League champions.

He had started the second game of the 1956 Series and lasted only one inning plus as the Dodgers bombed his offerings, scoring six times in the two innings he worked. Back after three days' rest, Larsen faced Dodger pitcher Sal Maglie. Delivering from a no-windup position, he set the Dodgers down 1-2-3 for nine innings. And only the second batter up, Pee Wee Reese, took Larsen to three balls before being called out on a fast ball.

The only other Dodgers who threatened Larsen's perfect game were Jackie Robinson, who hit a vicious grounder in the second inning off third baseman Andy Carey's glove that was retrieved quickly by Gil McDougald for the put-out; Gil Hodges, who hit a screaming line drive that center fielder Mickey Mantle caught on the run in the fifth; and Sandy Amaros, who blasted a long drive that barely went foul in the fifth inning. But when Larsen threw a third strike past the last batter—pinch hitter Dale Mitchell—and plate umpire Babe Pinella raised his right arm, Larsen had his perfect game.

*How many rookies have started—and won—the first game of a World Series?*

In the 72 World Series played through 1980, over 120 pitchers pitching in their first full season in the major leagues have been brought in to pitch, but only four rookies have ever started *and won* the opening game of a Series: Babe Adams in 1909, Spec Shea in 1947, Joe Black in 1952 and Bob Walk of the Phillies in 1980. No less than 33 rookies have started games in the Series, and 16 have won their games. But only five have ever been tapped to pitch the opening game—Babe Adams in 1909 for the Pirates, Paul Derringer in 1931 for the Cardinals, Spec Shea in 1947 for the Yankees, Don Newcombe in 1949 for the Dodgers and Joe Black in 1952 for the Dodgers. And only Adams, Shea and Black won their post-season debuts, with Adams winning three times in the 1909 Series, Shea twice in 1947 and Black losing twice after his opening-game victory.

*Name the only four players to win World Series games 1–0 by virtue of their solo home runs.*

Four times a team has won a World Series game 1–0 by virtue of a home run, and twice it happened in one Series. The four players whose solo homers decided a game are: Casey Stengel, who hit a seventh-inning home run for the Giants to beat the Yankees in the third game of the 1923 Series; Tommy Henrich, whose bottom-of-the-ninth homer beat the Dodgers, and Newcombe for the Yankees in the opening game of the 1949 Series; and Paul Blair and Frank Robinson, who hit solo home runs in the third and fourth games of the 1966 Series, enabling the Orioles to sweep the Dodgers.

*Who hit the first World Series home run by a pitcher?*

Cleveland's Jim Bagby, Sr., hit the first World Series home run ever hit by a pitcher. It happened in the fifth game of the 1920 World Series, a Series that was also memorable for the first grand-slam home run ever hit and the only unassisted triple play ever executed. Since then ten pitchers have hit World Series home runs, with Bob Gibson and Dave McNally hitting two and McNally hitting the only grand slammer ever by a pitcher.

*Name the only father-and-son team to appear in two World Series each.*

There have been many father-and-son teams, and some have played in at least one World Series each, but the only father and son to each play in two World Series are the Hegans, with father Jim catching in the 1948 and 1954 fall classics for Cleveland and son Mike pinch-hitting one time in the 1964 Series for the Yankees and playing first base for the 1972 Oakland A's.

Other father-and-son duos to appear in the World Series are the Sullivans (Billy, Sr., caught in the 1906 Series for the White Sox, and Billy, Jr., caught in the 1940 Series for the Tigers); the Bagbys (Jim, Sr., pitched in the 1920 Series for the Indians and Jim, Jr., pitched in the 1946 Series for the Red Sox); and the Johnsons (Ernie was a utility infielder for the 1923 Yankees and son Don played second base for the 1945 Cubs).

*Who was the only pitcher to appear in all seven games of a seven-game World Series?*

Darold Knowles pitched in all seven games of the 1973 World Series for the Oakland A's, although he only pitched 6⅓ innings in all seven of his appearances against the New York Mets. Knowles allowed four hits, walked five and struck out five in posting an 0.00 ERA with two saves.

*Who was the youngest pitcher to complete a World Series game? The youngest to ever throw a shutout?*

The youngest pitcher ever to complete a game in the Series was "Bullet" Joe Bush of the Philadelphia A's, who was only 20 years, 10 months and 12 days old when he went the distance to beat the New York Giants 8–2 in the third game of the 1913 Series. The youngest ever to throw a shutout was Jim Palmer of the Baltimore Orioles, who beat the Los Angeles Dodgers—and Sandy Koufax—6–0 in the second game of the 1966 Series at the tender young age of 20 years, 11 months and 21 days.

*Name the only four black pitchers to ever win a World Series game.*

Only four black pitchers have won games in the World Series, but one of them, Bob Gibson of the St. Louis Cardinals, holds several World Series records, including most games won in a row, with seven, and most strikeouts, with 17 in the first game of the 1968 Series. The other three are Joe Black, who won the first game of the 1952 Series for Brooklyn; Jim "Mudcat" Grant, who won the first and sixth games of the 1965 Series for the Minnesota Twins; and John Wyatt, who won the sixth game of the 1967 Series for the Boston Red Sox in relief.

*Who set a World Series record one year and tied it the next?*

The only World Series record equaled by the same player the year after he set it was the base-stealing record. Lou

Brock set it with seven thefts in a seven-game Series in 1967, and equaled it the very next year.

*Who holds the record for hitting safely in the most consecutive World Series games?*

Hank Bauer hit safely in 17 consecutive games in World Series play, including all seven games of the 1956 and 1957 Series and the first three of the 1958 Series. The only other player to hit in all seven games of two consecutive World Series in which he appeared was Roberto Clemente, who hit in all seven games of the 1960 Series and all seven of the 1971 Series for 14 consecutive games in which he hit safely.

*Name the four pitchers who have pitched one-hitters in the World Series.*

Everyone remembers Don Larsen's perfect game in the 1956 Series, but somehow forgotten are the one-hitters thrown by Ed Reulbach for the Cubs against the White Sox in the 1906 Series, by Claude Passeau for the Cubs against the Tigers in the 1945 Series, by Floyd "Bill" Bevens for the Yankees in the 1947 Series against the Dodgers and by Jim Lonborg of the Red Sox against the Cardinals in the 1967 Series. The four hitters who "spoiled" the bids of these four pitchers for no-hitters were Jiggs Donahue in 1906, Rudy York in 1945, Cookie Lavagetto in 1947 and Julian Javier in 1967.

*What player played on five pennant-winning teams in his first five years in the majors?*

Charlie Silvera, backup catcher for the New York Yankees behind Yogi Berra for his entire career, played for the 1949, 1950, 1951, 1952 and 1953 Yankee teams that each won pennants in his first five full seasons in the majors.

Although eligible for each of the five fall classics, and two others in 1955 and 1956, Silvera only saw action in one game out of the 42 in which he was eligible to play, coming to bat twice with no hits to show for his performance.

*Who was the oldest man to appear in a World Series game? The youngest?*

Jack Quinn, who pitched two innings in the third game of the 1930 World Series for the Philadelphia A's against the St. Louis Cardinals, was the oldest player to appear in a World Series game, pitching two innings and allowing three hits and one run, at the age of 46 years and 3 months. The youngest player ever appear in a World Series game was Freddie Lindstrom, who at the age of 18 years and 10 months played all seven games of the 1924 World Series at third base for the New York Giants. Lindstrom is best remembered in the 1924 Series as the fielder over whose head Earl McNeely's easy grounder hopped after hitting a pebble for the Series-winning hit.

*What player played the longest time in the majors before playing in a World Series game?*

Walter Johnson, "The Big Train," waited 18 years for his first chance to appear in a World Series game, in 1924. Johnson, who had come up in 1907 as a raw rookie who was discovered pitching in a small league in Idaho, pitched 21 years for the Washington Senators, most of them for a second-division club. But when playing manager Bucky Harris brought the Senators their first pennant in 1924, Johnson responded by winning the final game of the seven-game Series against the Giants, 18 years after he broke in.

*Name the only five pitchers to win two games in a four-game Series.*

Only five pitchers have won two games in a four-game Series, two in the same Series. The five are Bill James and Dick Rudolph, who each won two games in the 1914 Miracle Braves' sweep of the A's; Waite Hoyt, who won two in the 1928 Yankees' sweep of the Cardinals; Red Ruffing, who won a pair from the Cubs in 1938; and Sandy Koufax, who won two from the Yankees in 1963 for the Dodgers.

*Name the only player to hit home runs in his first two times up in the World Series.*

Several players have hit home runs their first time up in the World Series, but only Gene Tenace, Oakland A's catcher and first baseman in the 1972 Series, hit two in his first two times up in Series competition. Tenace, Oakland's second-string catcher during the regular season, drove in nine runs and tied the World Series record with four homers in the '72 classic, and two of them were in his first two times up. He also made World Series history by being the first player with a hairpiece to play in the Series.

*Who played right field for the New York Yankees in the 1942 World Series?*

When regular right fielder Tommy Henrich went into the service during the 1942 season, after playing in 127 games, the Yankees picked up outfielder Roy Cullenbine from the Washington Senators on waivers. Cullenbine hit .364 in the 27 games he played for the Yankees after he joined them on August 31, and also played all five games of the 1942 World Series in right field for the New York Yankees, batting .263 with five hits in 19 times at bat. The Yankees lost in five to the St. Louis Cardinals—Joe McCarthy's only World Series loss as manager of the Yankees.

*Who hit the first grand-slam home run for a National League team in the Series?*

American Leaguers have hit ten grand-slam homers in World Series play—starting with Elmer Smith's four-run blast in the fifth game of the 1920 Series for Cleveland— and New York Yankee members have been responsible for no less than seven of them. The National League has only had two grand-slammers, the first coming in the fourth game of the 1962 Series, hit by Chuck Hiller, the second baseman for the San Francisco Giants, and the second one hit in the 1964 Series, hit by Ken Boyer, third baseman for the St. Louis Cardinals, both appropriately enough hit against the New York Yankees. (Boyer's blast, in the fourth game, was the only one of the 12 grand-slammers to produce *all* of his team's runs in a winning cause, giving the Cards a 4–3 victory over the Yankees.)

*What pitcher gave up the first home run in World Series play?*

Cy Young, the winningest pitcher in baseball history, was the starting pitcher in the first game of the first World Series ever held between the two leagues, in 1903. But Young, pitching for the Red Sox, was touched for seven runs and 12 hits by the Pittsburgh Pirates, including Pirate third baseman Tommy Leach's first hit ever in World Series play in the first inning and the first home run ever hit in the Series by Pittsburgh's outfielder Jimmy Sebring in the seventh. Sebring's ball got past Boston outfielder Chick Stahl and stopped just short of the overflow crowd, as Stahl, according to one report, "quit on Sebring's hit."

*What National League player had the highest World Series slugging average for one Series?*

Lou Gehrig and Babe Ruth both had slugging averages of over 1.000 in two Series each (Gehrig 1.727 in 1928 and 1.118 in 1932, and Ruth 1.000 in 1923 and 1.375 in 1928), but the National League record is 1.071, a mark set by Donn Clendenon in the 1969 Series. Clendenon had three home runs, a double and a single in 14 times at bat to set the all-time National League record for World Series slugging average.

*What player accounted for five outs in World Series play in only two at bats?*

Brooklyn pitcher Clarence Mitchell came up to bat twice in the fifth game of the 1920 World Series and in those two at bats accounted for five outs. He achieved this distinction by lining to Cleveland second baseman Bill Wambsganss in the fifth for the only unassisted triple play in World Series history, and then two innings later grounding into a rally-ending double play that again included Wambsganss. Mitchell had come into the game in relief of Brooklyn starter Burleigh Grimes, who five years later was to suffer through an ordeal similar to Mitchell's. One afternoon in 1925 Grimes went to bat three times and hit into two double plays and one triple play.

*What three men were on the most losing World Series teams?*

According to baseball's book of official records, both Harold "Pee Wee" Reese and Elston Howard played for six World Series losers. Reese, in seven Series for the Brooklyn Dodgers, was on the losing side every time but once—in 1955—losing to the Yankees in 1941, 1947, 1949, 1952, 1953 and 1956. Howard was on the winning side in 1956, 1958, 1961 and 1962 as a member of the New York Yankees and on the losing side in 1955, 1957, 1960, 1963 and 1964 as a Yankee and in 1967 playing with the Boston Red Sox.

The third man? It was John McGraw, the second most winning manager of all time, but the loser of six of the nine World Series the New York Giants played under his aegis—in 1911, 1912, 1913, 1917, 1923 and 1924. Mc-

Graw compiled the unenviable record of suffering the most World Series defeats ever by a manager, with a total of 28 lost games in his seven World Series appearances.

*Name the only modern player to play in a World Series game without having played in a regular season game that same year.*

World War II strained the very fabric of big-league baseball. Over 250 men went into the armed services or into essential war-related work in war plants. And by the fourth year of the war, teams starved for manpower were reduced to putting ads in newspapers advertising openings on their farm clubs for anyone with previous professional experience. To fill up their rosters, clubs resorted to signing up anyone who could reasonably impersonate a player. Washington signed up a player who had starred with the New York Department of Sanitation team, and the St. Louis Browns brought up a one-armed player named Pete Wyshner (Pete "Gray") to play the outfield.

But then came V-J Day and the veterans came back as fast as they could be mustered out. Baseball waived its traditional rule that only those players who had been on the rosters on September 1 were eligible to play in the World Series. In the 1945 Series, the Chicago Cubs were pitted against the Detroit Tigers, who won the American League pennant when Hank Greenberg celebrated his 50-month absence from the diamond by hitting a last-day home run. One of the returning Cubs was catcher Clyde McCullough, who had come back too late to participate in regular season play but was allowed to play in the World Series. McCullough came to bat once as a pinch hitter in the 1945 Series, becoming the only modern player to play in a World Series game but not in a regular season contest.

One other player, named Holliday, played in the 1885 "World Series" but not in a regular season game that year. In the fourth game of the 1885 World Series (on October 17, 1885) between the Chicago Nationals and St. Louis

Browns of the American Association, Holliday (thought by many to be "Bug" Holliday who came from St. Louis) played right field, going 0 for 4. The regular center fielder, George Gore, had gotten into the bad graces of manager Cap Anson, who dismissed him after the first game and used Clarkson and Silver Flint (pitcher and catcher) in right field in the second and third games before drafting Holliday.

*Name the only players to hit World Series homers in each league.*

Only four players have hit World Series homers while playing on teams in both the American and National Leagues. The first of the quartet was Enos Slaughter, who hit homers in both the 1942 and 1946 Series for the Cards and in the 1956 Series for the New York Yankees. The next to hit round-trippers in the Series for teams in both leagues was Bill Skowron, who hit seven Series homers for the Yankees in the 1955, 1956, 1958, 1960 and 1961 Series and also hit one for the Los Angeles Dodgers in the 1963 Series against the Yankees. Another Yankee, Roger Maris, hit home runs in the 1960, 1961 and 1962 Series for the Bronx Bombers and then hit one for the Cardinals in the 1967 Series. And the fourth man to hit home runs in each league was Frank Robinson, who hit a home run for Cincinnati in the 1961 Series and seven more for the Baltimore Orioles in the 1966, 1969, 1970 and 1971 Series.

## 6TH INNING

# THE ALL-STAR GAME

*Name the only player to hit home runs for both sides in All-Star games.*

The only man to hit homers for both the American League and the National League is Frank Robinson, who hit a home run in the second 1959 All-Star game for the National League and a home run in the 1971 All-Star game for the American League, the only two he hit in All-Star competition.

*Who was the only pitcher to start two All-Star games in the same year?*

The All-Star game became the All-Star games for four years, 1959 through 1962. And in the two games played in 1959 Don Drysdale of the Los Angeles Dodgers started both games for the National League, losing one and not figuring in the decision in the other.

*Who was the starting pitcher for one of the two leagues in the All-Star game for five of the first six years?*

Vernon "Lefty" Gomez, star pitcher for the New York Yankees teams of the Thirties, started five of the first six All-Star games for the American League. He won the first game in 1933, the third game in 1935 and the fifth game in 1937 and lost the sixth game in 1938, the last All-Star game he ever appeared in.

*Name the only three non—Cincinnati Reds on the starting 1957 National League All-Star team.*

An avalanche of votes from Cincinnati elected a starting team of eight Cincinnati Reds for the National League's 1957 All-Star team. But Baseball Commissioner Ford Frick disallowed the bulk votes that came in at the last minute and named three players who had been ahead before the final deluge of votes poured in.

Named to the team, although finishing second in the voting, were Stan Musial at first, Willie Mays in center field and Hank Aaron in right field. They joined five Cincinnati Reds who had already been elected before the last-minute votes: Johnny Temple at second, Don Hoak at third, Roy McMillan at short, Frank Robinson in left and Ed Bailey as the catcher in the starting lineup. Three other Reds were moved out of the starting lineup by the commissioner's edict to make room for Musial, Mays and Aaron. They were George Crowe, the first baseman; Gus Bell, the center fielder; and Wally Post, the right fielder.

*What pitcher was the official winning pitcher in an All-Star game although he did not retire one batter?*

Dean Stone, of the Washington Senators, came in to relieve Chicago's Bob Keegan in the eighth inning of the 1954 All-Star game with Red Schoendienst on third and Alvin Dark on first, two out and the score 9–8 in favor of the National League. The first batter to face Stone was Brooklyn's Duke Snider, who took the first two pitches, one wide for a ball and one for a strike.

With the count 1-1, Schoendienst tried to steal home and was tagged out by American League catcher Yogi Berra, although the base-line coaches Leo Durocher and Charley Grimm claimed Stone had committed a balk. Then, when the American League scored three runs in the bottom of the eighth, Stone, who had been replaced in the ninth by Virgil Trucks, became the official winner, although he had only thrown two pitches and not officially retired one batter.

*Name the five American League stars that Carl Hubbell struck out in a row in the 1934 All-Star game.*

The 1934 All-Star game, held appropriately enough at the Polo Grounds, home of the New York Giants, was the scene of one of the greatest pitching feats of All-Star game history—if not all-time baseball history—by New York Giants pitcher Carl Hubbell.

After Detroit's Charlie Gehringer had led off the game with a single and Washington's Heinie Manush had walked, Hubbell bore down to get Babe Ruth on a called third strike, struck out Gehrig swinging and also struck out the A's' Jimmie Foxx, who missed one of Hubbell's screwballs.

He opened the second by striking out Chicago's Al Simmons and the playing manager for the American League All Stars, Washington's Joe Cronin, to complete his unprecedented and unequaled string of five strikeouts in a row. Then, after the Yankee's Bill Dickey had reached him for a single, Hubbell struck out Yankee pitcher Lefty Gomez to make it six strikeouts in the first two innings.

*Who hit the first All-Star home run for the National League?*

Everyone remembers that Babe Ruth hit the first home run in All-Star competition, hitting one in the third inning of the first All-Star game in history in Chicago in 1933 as part of their "Century of Progress" celebration. But few remember that Frankie Frisch, the playing manager of the St. Louis Cardinals, stroked the National League's first All-Star homer just three innings later, the National League's last run in a 4–2 losing cause. Frisch also hit the National League's second All-Star-game home run the following year, hitting one of Lefty Gomez's offerings in the first inning of the 1934 game, again with nobody on base and again in a losing cause.

*Who were the only two players named to starting All-Star teams at three different positions?*

Many players have been selected at two different positions on All-Star teams, but, counting the outfield as one position, only two men—Harmon Killebrew and Pete Rose—have ever been elected to the starting team at three different positions. Harmon Killebrew of the Washington Senators and Minnesota Twins made it into the All-Star game as a third baseman (in 1959, 1961, 1966, 1969 and 1970), an outfielder (in 1963 and 1964), and a first baseman (in 1965, 1967, 1968 and 1971), starting at least one game at each position. His versatile performance was matched in 1976 by Cincinnati's Pete Rose, who made it into the All-Star Game for the ninth time, but his first as a third baseman, adding it to his two times as a second baseman and his six times as an outfielder.

*How many grand-slam home runs have been hit in All-Star play?*

With almost 100 home runs hit in the history of the All-Star game, there has not been one grand-slam home run among them.

*Name the only player to go to bat over 20 times in World Series and All-Star games and go hitless.*

Wally Berger, who came up to the Boston Braves in 1930 as a home-run-hitting outfielder—setting the rookie mark for most home runs hit in the first year with 38—went to bat 26 times in seven World Series games and three All-Star games and couldn't buy a hit. Berger pinch-hit three times in the 1937 Series for the New York Giants and played all four games for the 1939 Cincinnati Reds and failed in 18 attempts to get a hit. Named as a starting outfielder for the National League squad in the 1933, '34 and '35 All-Star games, he went for the collar in eight more at bats to give him an 0-26 record in World Series and All-Star play, an all-time record for batting futility.

> *What player hit the other two home runs in the All-Star game won by Ted Williams's ninth-inning homer?*

Ted Williams brought the American League back from a 5—4 deficit and sure defeat with a three-run homer in the bottom of the ninth to beat the National League 7–5 in the 1941 All-Star game at Detroit's Briggs Stadium. But the National League star of the ninth annual All-Star game was Pittsburgh Pirate shortstop Arky Vaughan. He had three hits in four trips to the plate, including two two-run homers to account for four of the National League's five runs, and set an All-Star-game record for homers.

The only other players to hit two homers in an All-Star game, tying Vaughan for the most round-trippers in one All-Star game, are Ted Williams, who did it in the 1946 game, Al Rosen in the 1954 game and Willie McCovey, who belted two in the 1969 "Baseball Centennial" All-Star game.

> *Who drove in the first run in All-Star-game competition?*

Vernon "Lefty" Gomez only drove in 62 runs in 14 years of regular season and World Series play, plus one more in All-Star competition. But the one he drove in in All-Star play was the very first RBI in All-Star-game history, coming in the second inning of the first All-Star game, held in Chicago on July 6, 1933. "Wild" Bill Hallahan, the Cardinal pitching ace, got Al Simmons out to start the second, then walked Jimmy Dykes and Joe Cronin. After retiring catcher Rick Ferrell, the weak-hitting Gomez came up and rifled a single to center to score Dykes with the first RBI in All-Star competition.

*Who is the youngest player ever to play in an All-Star game?*

When Minnesota Twins catcher Butch Wynegar batted for pitcher Luis Tiant in the seventh inning of the 1976 All-Star game and walked, he became the youngest player ever to get into an All-Star game, at the age of 20 years and 4 months old. The youngest player to play in an All-Star game before Wynegar was Baltimore pitcher Jerry Walker, who, at the tender age of 20 years and 5 months, started and won the second 1959 All-Star game.

# 7TH INNING

---

# 7TH-INNING STRETCH

*Who was the only player to be thrown out of a major-league game but never play in one?*

On September 27, 1951, the Brooklyn Dodgers were playing in Boston and trying to protect their fast-shrinking lead over the onrushing New York Giants. With the score 3–3 in the bottom of the eighth, Jackie Robinson cleanly fielded a ground ball and fired it home to catcher Roy Campanella in an attempt to get the Braves' Bob Addis, who had been at third. But plate umpire Frank Dascoli called Addis safe with the Braves' fourth and winning run and an argument ensued. First Campanella, then coach Cookie Lavagetto and finally the entire Dodger bench were thrown out of the game by Dascoli for continuing the argument.

One of those 15 cleaned out of the Dodgers' dugout by Dascoli was a young outfielder named Bill Sharman, just up from Ft. Worth, where he had hit .286. Sharman, who later went on to basketball fame in Boston, never appeared in a major-league game, playing just one more year in the minors with St. Paul. But he's an interesting footnote to history as the only player ever to be thrown out of a big-league game without having played in one.

*Who holds the record for the most times caught stealing in one year?*

When Ty Cobb stole 96 bases in 1915, for the then record, he was also caught stealing a record 38 times. The National League record for most times caught stealing is held by Miller Huggins, the St. Louis Cardinals' second baseman, who was caught stealing 36 times in 68 attempts in 1914. On the more successful side of base thievery, Max Carey, Pittsburgh outfielder, was the most successful burglar in modern times, stealing 51 bases in 53 attempts in 1922, and Davey Lopes had 38 successful steals in succession in 1975 to set the consecutive-theft mark. The record for the most steals in a season without being caught was 11, stolen by Johnny Bench in 1975.

*What player has appeared on the number-one card in
the Topps annual gum-card set the most times?*

Since Topps first started issuing its bubble-gum cards in
1951, Hank Aaron has appeared on the number-one card
more times than any other player—five years. And one
player, Marshall Bridges, holds the record for playing the
most years *without* appearing on a card—seven years.

*What bat set two National League records—13 years
apart?*

After Johnny Frederick set his all-time record for the most
pinch-hit home runs in one year with six, the bat he set the
record with was kept by his old Brooklyn Dodgers teammate, Del Bissonette, in the attic of his Winthrop, Maine,
house. When Bissonette came back to coach and manage
the Boston Braves in 1945, he exhumed Frederick's old
bat and loaned it to Braves star Tommy Holmes, who
used the record-breaking bat to set the modern National
League record for hitting in 37 consecutive games.

Del Bissonette also gained some notoriety by being the
subject of L. H. Addington's famous baseball limerick:

> The Dodgers have Del Bissonette,
> No meal has he ever missed yet;
> The question that rises
> Is one that surprises,
> Who paid for all Del Bissonette?

*Who scored major-league baseball's one millionth
run?*

Houston Astro outfielder Bob Watson scored on teammate
Milt May's homer at 12:32 P.M. on May 6, 1975, to win
one million pennies for himself and his teammates, a Toot-
sie Rolls promotion conceived by New York publicist Ted
Worner for the player scoring the one millionth run. Wat-

son, who had walked in the second inning of a game played against the Giants at Candlestick Park in San Francisco, scored just three seconds before Dave Concepcion hit a home run in Cincinnati against the Braves and scored run one million and one.

*Who was the only player ever to hit the Astrodome roof?*

Ed Roebuck, renowned as much for his fungo hitting as for his relief pitching, hit a ball with a fungo bat 190 feet into the air, striking an Astrodome girder high above first base before a game between the Astros and the Phillies on September 14, 1964.

The only other player to come close to hitting the Astrodome roof was also a Philly, and it occurred during a game, not during batting practice. On June 10, 1974, Mike Schmidt blasted a ball that hit the public-address system hanging from the Astrodome roof 300 feet from home plate and 117 feet above the playing field. Under the Astrodome ground rules, the ball was still in play and, with runners on, Schmidt had to settle for a single—the longest single in baseball history.

*Name the only three men to catch baseballs dropped from the Washington Monument.*

Just eight years after the Washington Monument was opened to the public in 1886, a ball was caught that had been dropped from the observation deck 504 feet above the street to settle a monumental argument. The argument was between Adrian "Cap" Anson and the chief clerk of the Arlington Hotel, where the Chicago White Stockings of the old National League were quartered, and the issue was whether any "baseballist on earth ever had or ever could catch a ball dropped from the Washington Monument."

On August 25, 1894, Anson deputized catcher William F. "Pop" Schriver to position himself at the base of the monument and his star pitcher, Clark Griffith, to go up to the observation deck and lob a ball down to him to settle the argument. As they had done so many times during the season, Griffith connected with his batterymate, and a new "sport"—height catching—was started.

Fourteen years later, on August 21, 1908, another argument between two Washington "clubmen" (a euphemism for sportsmen) culminated in the second successful attempt to catch a ball dropped from the monument. The two bet $500 on whether Washington Senator catcher Charles "Gabby" Street could catch a ball dropped from 504 feet above "Street" level; and, armed with a basket of baseballs and a chute, the two clubmen ascended the monument to settle their wager.

Street's supporter, W. J. Preston Gibson, used the chute to send ten balls down in the general direction of Street, but none cleared the base of the monument. Discarding the chute and throwing them out himself, Gibson finally was able to get one in the general vicinity of Street; and on the lucky 13th toss, Street rewarded Gibson's faith in his abilities by circling under a ball and catching it.

Two years later, on August 24, 1910, Chicago White Sox catcher Billy Sullivan caught three of the 23 baseballs dropped from the observation deck by Chicago pitchers Ed Walsh and Doc White, becoming the third and last man to catch a ball dropped from the Washington Monument.

But trying for height records had become part of baseball. And during spring training at Daytona Beach in 1914, Brooklyn Dodger manager Wilbert Robinson, responding to a challenge, attempted to break the record of 504 feet by having a ball dropped to him from a plane flying at over 525 feet. Instead of dropping a baseball, however, aviatrix Ruth Law dropped a grapefruit. When Robinson missed the missile with his glove and stopped it with his chest, the grapefruit splattered all over him. Robinson, feeling the juice oozing over his prostrate body, thought he was soaked with blood; and when informed of the switch he at first suspected, with more than a little justification, that his player, the mischievous Casey Stengel, had done him in. Ms. Law later revealed that neither Stengel nor any of the other Dodgers had had a hand in substituting a grapefruit for the baseball. She said that when her Wright Model B plane, engaged by the merchants of Daytona Beach as a tourist attraction, had motored to the end of the runway as part of the stunt arranged by the town and the team, she found that she had "forgotten to bring along a ball." So, she explained, "a man who had brought a small grapefruit in his lunch suggested that I drop the grapefruit instead."

It wasn't until August 20, 1938, that the record for height catches was established. On that day, Cleveland Indians third baseman Ken Keltner dropped balls from the upper ledge of the Cleveland Terminal Tower, 675 feet above street level, to Indians catchers Frankie Pytlak and Hank Helf. One attempt was subsequently made to break the record: On August 3, 1939, San Francisco Seals catcher Joe Sprinz tried to catch a ball dropped from a blimp hovering 800 feet over Treasure Island, as part of San Francisco's International Golden Gate Exposition. But, although Sprinz got under the ball and momentarily held onto it, the force of the ball traveling at 217 feet a second drove the glove into his face, causing Sprinz to lose the ball and eight teeth with it, breaking his jaw, but not the height record.

*Who was the only Heisman Trophy winner to play major-league baseball?*

Vic Janowicz, the Ohio State halfback who won the Heisman Trophy in 1950 as the nation's outstanding collegiate football player, played 83 games for the Pittsburgh Pirates in 1953 and 1954 before returning to football, where he played two years with the Washington Redskins in 1954 and 1955. Janowicz's athletic career was cut short by a serious automobile accident in 1956.

*Name the only three men who have appeared in a
World Series game and a Rose Bowl game.*

The only three men to appear in both a World Series game
and a Rose Bowl game are Jackie Jensen, Chuck Essegian
and Earl "Greasy" Neale. Jensen, the only man to be both
an MVP in baseball and an All-American in football,
starred for California's Golden Bears in the 1949 Rose
Bowl and played in one game for the New York Yankees
in the 1950 World Series. Essegian, a member of Stanford's "Rug Merchants" who played in the 1952 Rose
Bowl, set a World Series record in the 1959 Series by hitting two home runs as a pinch hitter. Neale, who led the
Cincinnati Reds in batting in the ill-fated 1919 World
Series, coached the little Washington and Jefferson College
(enrollment 250 students) team which went to the 1922
Rose Bowl and tied a powerful California team 0–0.

Neale played football with Jim Thorpe and others on
weekends at Canton during the time he played the outfield
for the Reds, and served as coach of Washington and Jefferson in his "spare" time. He later coached at the University of Virginia, West Virginia University, the Portsmouth
Spartans in the fledgling NFL, and finally capped off his
coaching career as the coach of the champion Philadelphia
Eagles in 1948 and 1949.

*Who was Myrtle Power?*

Mrs. Myrtle Power, a 70-year-old grandmother, appeared
on "The $64,000 Question" in the summer of 1955 as an
expert on the subject of baseball. She answered ten questions asked of her by emcee Hal March and quit at the
$32,000 level, the highest in the program's short history
until it was tied by Gino Prado on opera and surpassed by
a marine captain whose subject was cooking. Here are the
ten questions asked of Mrs. Power, the last four of them in
an isolation booth to the accompaniment of syncopated
music, which we had trouble reproducing here:

$64: What is the keystone base?

$128: What is meant when a player is "on deck"?

$256: What is meant by a "duster"?

$512: What is meant by a "Texas Leaguer"?

$1000: A baseball manager dreams of a player who can hit safely every time he comes to bat. The record for batting safely—successive times at bat—stands at 12. Two men hold that record: Walt Dropo, who hit 12 successive times for Detroit in 1952, and one other man. For $1000 name the other man who shares the record for successive hits since 1900.

$2000: Bob Feller is the only pitcher to pitch three no-hitters, but there are a number of pitchers who have pitched two no-hitters. Allie Reynolds is one. For $2000 name a pitcher who pitched for Detroit and a pitcher who pitched for Cincinnati, both having two no-hitters to their credit.

$4000: Babe Ruth leads all other batters in home runs during a season. His major-league record is 60 homers in 1927. Two other major-league batters are tied for second place, having hit the same number of homers each, though in two different years. Now, for $4000, I want three things—the names of the two batters, and the number of homers each hit.

$8000: The St. Louis Cardinals have won the National League pennant at least nine times. Give me the exact dates of the last four times the Cardinals won the pennant. You can give the four dates in any order you please.

$16,000: One of baseball's all-time highlights took place in the 1934 All-Star game when Carl Hubbell struck out five men in a row. The brilliance of this performance can be measured by averaging the hitting record of those five American League sluggers. It comes to .332. Now, for $16,000, name the five men struck out in succession by Carl Hubbell in the 1934 All-Star game. You can list them in any order.

$32,000:  The official record books list seven players who are credited with over 3000 hits during their careers in the major leagues. Ty Cobb heads the list with 4191 hits garnered in his 24 years of play. Name the remaining six players who have a lifetime total of 3000 or more hits.

The answers Mrs. Power gave—all correct—were: $64 —Second base; $128—The next batter up; $256—A pitch thrown too close to the batter; $512—A looping hit, too far out for the infield and too close in for the outfield; $1000—Frank "Pinky" Higgins, with the Boston Red Sox in 1938; $2000—Virgil "Fire" Trucks of the Detroit Tigers and Johnny Vander Meer of the Cincinnati Reds (Ed. Note: In modern baseball, Cy Young and Larry Corcoran had three no-hitters *before* Feller.); $4000—Jimmie Foxx in 1932 and Hank Greenberg in 1938, 58 for each; $8000—1946, 1944, 1943 and 1942; $16,000— Babe Ruth, Lou Gehrig, Jimmie Foxx, Al Simmons and Joe Cronin; $32,000—Adrian "Cap" Anson, Honus Wagner, Napoleon "Nap" Lajoie, Tris Speaker, Eddie Collins and Paul Waner.

*Who played the female leads in* The Pride of the Yankees *and* The Babe Ruth Story?

*The Pride of the Yankees* was one of the all-time great tearjerkers, produced by Metro-Goldwyn-Mayer one year after the death of Lou Gehrig in 1941. It starred Gary Cooper as Gehrig and Teresa Wright as his wife, with supporting roles played by Walter Brennan, Dan Duryea and a 47-year-old neophyte named Babe Ruth, who played himself. The year that Babe Ruth died, 1948, *The Babe Ruth Story* was rushed out to market, starring in the title role a former minor-league ballplayer who had once been the batboy for the Yankees during the days when Ruth himself played for the Yankees, William Bendix, and Claire Trevor as Mrs. Clare Ruth, with Charles Bickford cast as Brother Mathias.

*Name the only man who ever participated on a major-league level in three sports.*

The "one-man gang" for Stanford, Ernie Nevers, played baseball, basketball and football professionally, the only man ever to participate in all three sports professionally at the major-league level. Nevers went directly from Stanford, where he had been an All-American fullback under Glenn "Pop" Warner in 1925, into the new National Football League in 1926. The blond, rugged-looking Nevers was the entire Duluth Eskimo franchise, passing from the double wing, drop-kicking field goals and tackling anyone who crossed his path with a relentless ferocity. Nevers, considered by many to be the greatest pro football player of all time, set the professional scoring record of 40 points in a single game against the Chicago Bears in 1929, scoring six touchdowns and four extra points, playing with the Chicago Cards, with whom he played through 1937.

His baseball career was not as noteworthy. Breaking in the year following his graduation, and the same year he started playing professional football, Nevers appeared in just 44 games for the St. Louis Cardinals as a pitcher in 1926, 1927 and 1928, winning six and losing 12. His greatest achievement in major-league baseball was serving up Babe Ruth's eighth and 41st home runs in 1927.

Nevers also played basketball for the Chicago Bruins in

the ABL for five games in the late Twenties. The Bruins were coached by George Halas, who himself played major-league baseball and football but never actually appeared in a basketball game professionally. Other near-three-sport men besides Halas include Ted Fritsch, who played football for the Green Bay Packers, basketball for the Oshkosh All-Stars in the ABL and baseball in the Pacific Coast League; and Connie Mack Berry, who played for the Detroit Lions, Cleveland Rams and Chicago Bears in the NFL, the Oshkosh All-Stars and in Triple-A baseball.

*Who was the only man to be a baseball player and manager and pro basketball player and head coach?*

While many athletes have combined pro baseball and pro basketball, among them Gene Conley, Dave DeBusschere, Chuck Conners and Del Rice, the only man to coach a professional basketball team and play pro basketball, as well as play and manage in major-league baseball, was Lou Boudreau. Boudreau, who played for and managed the Cleveland Indians and Boston Red Sox, as well as managing the Kansas City A's and the Chicago Cubs, played professional basketball with the Hammond Ciesar All-Americans in the NBL in the 1938–39 season.

Boudreau had been an All-Big-10 basketball player and had one more year of basketball eligibility left when the Cleveland Indians signed him, giving his mother the bonus so as not to harm his amateur standing. When the Big 10 found out, Boudreau was playing with the Hammond Ciesar team, which also included a guard named Johnny Wooden that year. The Indians, however, fearing for the safety of their prospective player, forbade him to continue playing professional basketball in the off-season, so the next year Hammond signed him to coach the team. But when the team lost four of its first five games, Boudreau was fired, returning to the diamond where he was destined for greatness.

One other big-league manager coached a professional basketball team in organized ball, but never played pro basketball. Red Rolfe, former great Yankee third baseman and future Detroit Tiger manager, coached the Toronto Huskies in the old BAA, winning 17 and losing 27 in 1946–47, the last of four coaches for the Huskies and their last coach ever—as they soon evaporated from the professional basketball landscape.

*Who served the longest as a coach in the major leagues?*

Nick Altrock, the old pitcher for the Chicago White Sox, coached the Washington Senators for 46 years, from 1912 through 1957, the longest tenure by far of any in major-league history. Coaches date back to 1909, when John McGraw put Arlie Latham on the base lines for the New York Giants. Before that, active players handled the coaching chores. Gradually staffs have developed to the point where there are now four or five coaches on most teams. A list of the longest-tenured coaches follows:

COACHES WHO HAVE SERVED THE LONGEST

| Yrs. | Coaches | Clubs Served | |
|------|---------|--------------|---|
| 46 | Nick Altrock | Senators | 1912–1957 |
| 26 | Frank Crosetti | 3 clubs | 1946–1971 |
| 23 | Jim Turner | 2 clubs | 1949–1973 |
| 23 | George Myatt | 5 clubs | 1950–1972 |
| 22 | Mel Harder | 5 clubs | 1947–1969 |
| 22 | Clyde Wares | Cards | 1930–35; 1937–52 |
| 21 | George Susce | 5 clubs | 1941–1972 |
| 21 | Johnny Cooney | 3 clubs | 1940–1964 |
| 21 | Tony Cuccinello | 4 clubs | 1949–1969 |
| 20 | Del Baker | 3 clubs | 1933–1960 |
| 20 | Ray Berres | Chi. Sox | 1949–66; 1968–69 |
| 19 | Art Fletcher | Yankees | 1927–1945 |
| 19 | Hans Wagner | Pirates | 1933–1951 |
| 18 | Hank Gowdy | 3 clubs | 1929–1948 |
| 18 | John Corriden | 4 clubs | 1932–1950 |

| Yrs. | Coaches | Clubs Served | |
|------|---------|--------------|------|
| 18 | John Schulte | 3 clubs | 1933–1950 |
| 18 | Earle Combs | 4 clubs | 1935–1954 |
| 18 | Benny Bengough | 3 clubs | 1940–1958 |

*Who was the first Little Leaguer to play major-league ball?*

The first graduate from the ranks of Little League ball, founded in Williamsport, Pennsylvania, in 1939, was Joey Jay, who came up to the Milwaukee Braves in 1953 as an 18-year-old pitcher.

The first to play in both a Little League World Series in Williamsport and a major-league World Series was John Wesley "Boog" Powell, who represented a team from Lakeland, Florida, in the Little League Series and the Baltimore Orioles in the major-league version.

*Who was the only ballplayer to have a brand of cigarettes named after him?*

American Tobacco, who also made Home Run cigarettes, came out with a "Ty Cobb" brand, whose slogan was "King of the Smoking Tobacco World," back in 1909 and 1910. The Ty Cobb brand was one of 16 different brands put out by the American Tobacco trust, which also issued cards of baseball players with every brand.

It was one of these cards that Cobb's 1909 World Series adversary, Honus Wagner, objected to, obtaining an injunction in court on the grounds that he didn't smoke and requesting that the cards of him issued on cigarette packs be removed from the market. There are so few of the Wagner cards still in existence that the going price for one is now $1800.

*What president of the United States attended the most baseball games while in office?*

Since the days of William Howard Taft, who aspired to be a baseball player with his hometown Cincinnati Reds before he entered law and politics, every president, up through Ford, has attended at least one major-league ball game while in office. But even though some presidents may have been more avowed fans, Harry Truman showed up 16 times to watch the Washington Senators play, including every opening day while he was in office.

Eisenhower was in attendance at Griffith Stadium to see the Senators 11 times, and once traveled to Brooklyn to watch the Dodgers beat the Yankees in the first game of the 1956 World Series.

Franklin Roosevelt threw out the first pitch of the season eight times and saw one of the games of the 1933 World Series in Washington, one of the games of the 1936 Series at the Polo Grounds and the 1937 All-Star game in Washington.

Herbert Hoover attended nine games, including throwing out the ceremonial first pitch in the four years he was in the White House and attending the 1930 and 1931 World Series, where he was booed by fans chanting the antiprohibition slogan "Beer, beer, beer."

Nixon attended 11 games, including eight in Washington—where he saw the only triple play ever seen in person by any president. It was Detroit versus Washington on the night of July 15, 1969. He also attended two regular season National League games in Anaheim in 1970 and 1973— the first president since Taft to see a regular season National League game.

Kennedy saw four, including the three openers when he was in office and the 1962 All-Star game.

Harding saw four, including the three openers in Washington while he was in the White House and one game at newly dedicated Yankee Stadium in 1923.

Coolidge saw nine, including four openers and three World Series games.

Lyndon Johnson saw three.

Taft, who started it all, saw 14 games, including regular season National League games in Pittsburgh, Cincinnati, Chicago and St. Louis, where he went to see a portion of both the Cardinals' and the Browns' games on the same afternoon, May 4, 1910, when both were playing at home.

Gerald Ford attended only two major-league games while in office—the 1976 Texas Ranger opener and the 1976 All-Star game in Philadelphia—largely because he is a football fan and no major-league baseball team is in attendance in Washington. And Jimmy Carter threw out the first ball at the seventh and deciding game of the 1979 World Series at Baltimore, bringing the Orioles the usual Carter luck. They lost the game, and the Series.

*When did Pepper Martin play for the Brooklyn Dodgers?*

Pepper Martin, "The Wild Horse of the Osage," played 13 years, coming up in 1928 for 39 games and then back up in 1930 to stay through 1940, adding a short footnote to his playing career in 1944 after managing in Triple-A ball for three years—all for the St. Louis Cardinals. Then, in 1948, at the age of 48, Martin was signed by Branch Rickey to scout for the Brooklyn Dodgers baseball team and play for the Brooklyn Dodgers football team in the All-American Football Conference as a kicker. But even Martin's presence couldn't bring the fans out, and by the end of the year Rickey and the owners of the Dodgers baseball team had turned the football franchise back to the league, ending a noble experiment and Martin's career as a Dodger.

*What's the name of the right fielder in Abbott and Costello's "Who's on First?" skit?*

First introduced in the 1945 Universal movie *The Naughty Nineties,* the "Who's on First?" vaudeville skit became as much a part of baseball as it did of Abbott and Costello's routine. In the skit, Bud Abbott, as Dexter Broadhurst, manager of the Wolves, tries to answer the questions of the inquisitive peanut vendor, Sebastian Dinwiddie, played by Lou Costello. And the answer to *"What*'s the name of the right fielder?" would *not* be "What," because What was the second baseman. In fact, there was no right fielder mentioned in the skit.

Besides second baseman What, the other members of this confusing but memorable team were: first base, Who; shortstop, I Don't Care; left field, Why; center field, Because; pitching, Tomorrow; catching, Today.

So the answer to this question can be either "What's on second" or that there was no right fielder. But it's not "I don't know," because now you've named the third baseman!

> *When was the first night baseball game in a major-league park?*

On August 28, 1910, a crowd of over 20,000 gathered at the then new White Sox Park to watch a night baseball game between two local nines, Logan Square and Rogers Park. Twenty 137,000-candlepower arc lights "made the diamond bright as day" and provided a preview for the first night game between two major-league teams—the Reds and the Phillies in Cincinnati's Redland Field on May 25, 1935.

> *What ballplayer was immortalized in a Pulitzer Prize–winning novel?*

The old fisherman in Ernest Hemingway's *Old Man and the Sea,* with plenty of time on his hands, is given to ruminating. One thought that crosses his mind as he waits for his own strike is how "the great DiMaggio" would have handled this situation. Ironically, Joe DiMaggio did little, if any, deep-sea fishing of this variety. Nonetheless his name had the right ring and his fame was a known quantity that could be played off of, much as it was in the song written by Simon and Garfunkel some 15 years later which, though entitled "Mrs. Robinson," asked the question, "Where Have You Gone, Joe DiMaggio?"

### Who preceded Casey at the bat?

In Ernest Thayer's immortal opus, written in 1888 and introduced by De Wolf Hopper, Casey is preceded by two men—Flynn and Blake (to rhyme with cake). And with Cooney and Barrows already out, these two needed to get on base for Casey to have a chance to pull the game out for Mudville, which was on the short end of a 4–2 score. The two verses in which Blake appears might refresh your memory as to how Casey was able to get up to bat.

> But Flynn preceded Casey, as did also Jimmy Blake,
> And the former was a lulu and the latter was a cake;
> So upon the stricken multitude grim melancholy sat,
> For there seemed but little chance of Casey's getting
>     to the bat.
>
> But Flynn let drive a single, to the wonderment of all,
> And Blake, the much despised, tore the cover off the
>     ball;
> And when the dust had lifted and the men saw what
>     had occurred,
> There was Johnny safe at second and Flynn a-hug-
>     ging third.

But while it's clear that Blake preceded Casey, even the author is somewhat confused as to whether his first name was Jimmy or Johnny. But it didn't matter to the author or the audiences by the end anyway, 'cause "Mighty Casey ha[d] struck out."

*Who played for the Brooklyn Dodgers, the New York Rangers and the New York Knicks in the same year?*

Long a favorite among New York bar triviots, this question presupposes that the person who "played" was an active player. She wasn't. For the person who played for the Brooklyn Dodgers, New York Rangers and New York Knicks, all in one season, was Gladys Gooding, the organist, who entertained before, during and after the game for these three teams during the Forties and early Fifties.

Another trick question, which could be called a slow curve—and which is not bounded by the Hudson River—goes, "What Detroit native once played with both the Lions and the Tigers?" The answer, unfortunately, is Clyde Beatty, the famous animal trainer. Any other triviot seeking to throw such slow curves can do so at his own risk.

*What was the name of the Cleveland Indian fan who sat on a flagpole until the Indians won the pennant?*

The 1949 Cleveland Indians were attempting to repeat as American League champions and were running into stiff competition from the New York Yankees and the Boston Red Sox—so stiff that the faint-hearted had lost hope in their chances. But not Cleveland fan Charles Lupica.

In mid-May Lupica constructed a 20-foot flagpole with a four-foot platform high atop his drugstore and mounted it with the declared intention of remaining there until the Indians recaptured first place. For the next 117 days he remained on his flagpole while the Indians gave chase to the Yankees and the Red Sox, breaking "Shipwreck" Van Nolan's record of 71 days. But on September 25, with the Indians mathematically eliminated from the pennant race, Lupica dismounted to join in a funeral procession as the Indians buried their American League flag.

*What baseball player's brother was killed in the ring by Max Baer?*

Former Phillies and Dodgers first baseman Dolf Camilli's brother, fighting under the name of "Frankie Campbell," was knocked out and killed by the force of a crushing right hand thrown by Max Baer, "The Livermore Larruper," in the fifth round of a match billed as "The Heavyweight Championship of California," on August 25, 1930. Camilli, who played for 12 years with the Phillies and Dodgers, as well as the Cubs and Red Sox, had also considered a career in the ring, but abandoned it after his brother's tragic end.

Other brother acts that have spanned the two sports of baseball and boxing include "Gentleman" Jim Corbett and his brother, Joe. Joe pitched for the old Baltimore Orioles during the late 1890s and led them in wins in 1897. But that very same year brother Jim lost his heavyweight crown to Bob Fitzsimmons, and the unmerciful taunts of Oriole opponents soon drove Joe from the mound and from the game. Former Brooklyn Dodgers coach Jake Pitler's brother was the manager of Billy Conn, the almost heavyweight champion of the world, in the early Forties, having changed his name to "Johnny Ray."

Several players have pursued careers both in the ring and on the field. Art "The Great" Shires, the flamboyant White Sox first baseman of the late Twenties, once fought the Chicago Bears' behemoth center George Trafton for the "Sports' Heavyweight Championship" and knocked him out. Six months later Shires was matched against

Boston Braves catcher Al Spohrer, and knocked him out in the fourth round. After this 1930 bout to settle baseball's championship, Commissioner Landis forbade any more boxing bouts between active ballplayers, thus ending Shires's winning streak at two. By 1932 Shires, waived to the Braves, and Spohrer became teammates, bearing no enmity but many fond memories from being the only two active players ever to box professionally.

Chick Gandil, the first baseman for baseball's infamous "Black Sox" team of 1919, boxed professionally, but not during his playing days. And Billy Martin, the Yankees manager, fought many times in the San Francisco area, both as an amateur and for money, an art that came in handy during his many on-the-field brawls with the likes of Jim Brewer, Jimmy Piersall and Clint Courtney, among others.

*Name the only player given a leave from military service to play for a major-league team.*

The only player who received a special leave to play for a major-league team was Willard Roland Gaines, a career naval officer who took time off to pitch for the Washington Senators. The 23-year-old Gaines, nicknamed "Nemo" by his teammates, had never played major-league ball before. He pitched in just four-plus innings in four games for the 1921 Senators and posted a 0.00 ERA before going back to the service, never to play again.

*Who shot Eddie Waitkus?*

On the night of June 14, 1949, Philadelphia Phillies first baseman Eddie Waitkus received a note in his room at the Edgewater Beach Hotel in Chicago from a young woman he did not know named Ruth Steinhagen, who insisted on seeing him in her room "as soon as possible" because of "something extremely important" she wanted to discuss. Responding to the urgency of the note, Waitkus was shot in the chest with a secondhand rifle purchased just the day before by Miss Steinhagen. According to the psychiatrist's report to the felony court, Miss Steinhagen had a crush on Waitkus, had memorized his every move, made his number —number 36—her favorite number, and stated that every-one reminded her of Waitkus. She was adjudged to be "schizophrenic" and was committed to a mental institution where she could be "under constant surveillance."

Fortunately for Waitkus—and the Phillies—he recov-ered and came back in 1950 to hit .284, the highest average in the "Whiz Kids" infield, contributing to their winning the National League pennant.

Waitkus was the second player shot by a female admirer and the second one shot in Chicago. On July 6, 1932, Billy Jurges, the second-year shortstop for the pennant-bound Chicago Cubs, was shot and wounded at Chicago's Carlos Hotel by a show girl, Violet Popovich Valli. Miss Valli was freed on bail, and the case was subsequently dismissed for want of prosecution. Jurges recovered, con-tributing to the Cubs' 1932 pennant. In the World Series that year against the Yankees, Jurges got four hits, in-cluding one double, as the Cubs lost in four games to the Yankees—exactly the same performance that *both* Wait-kus and the Phillies achieved against the Yankees in the World Series following his convalescence.

> *In one of the most famous fights in recent years, whom did Joe Adcock chase off the mound and into the dugout?*

On the night of July 18, 1956, Joe Adcock, with seven home runs in the last nine games, came to bat in the bot-tom of the second facing New York Giants pitcher Ruben Gomez. Gomez's first pitch hit Adcock, and as he jogged down the base line rubbing his wrist, Adcock yelled something toward the mound. The Puerto Rican right-hander yelled something back, and suddenly Adcock charged the mound. Gomez froze for just a moment, then threw the ball at Adcock and raced toward the Giants' dugout. Adcock, hit in the thigh this time, raced after Gomez with all of the Braves in close pursuit. Gomez, who later said, "I run—I don't want him to break all my ribs," was thrown out of the game and taken from Milwaukee's County Stadium under police escort. He was later fined $250 and suspended for three days, and Adcock was fined $100.

Gomez never got over the incident, slipping to a record of seven wins and 17 losses that year, and although he came back with 15 wins in 1957, his best playing—if not fighting—days were behind him and he won only 15 games in five years after that.

### What player's face was insured for $100,000?

Johnny Berardino, who later changed his name to "Beradino" for acting purposes, had his face insured for $100,000 while playing second base for the St. Louis Browns in the early Fifties. Berardino, who went on to star in several daytime soaps, didn't want his face injured by any grounders or beanballs, and as a promotion gimmick St. Louis owner Bill Veeck took out an insurance policy on his features, later to grace many a television screen.

### Who appeared in the most consecutive games?

Bill McGowan, an American League umpire from 1925 through 1954, appeared in 2541 consecutive games over a period of 16½ years, far eclipsing Lou Gehrig's 2130 consecutive-game total.

*What two roommates had the shortest combined last names?*

There have been several players with only three letters in their last names—Mel Ott, Emil Yde, Joey Jay among them. But Billy Cox and Preacher Roe were two whose three-letter last names were combined not only as teammates but roommates during several years of their seven-year stay with the Dodgers, which started for both in 1948 and ended for both in 1954.

*Who was the first second-generation black player in the majors?*

Sam Hairston caught but four games for the Chicago White Sox in 1951, batting five times and collecting two hits. But as a scout for the Chicago White Sox organization today, he has had three more hits—his sons. His oldest son, Johnny Hairston, caught three games for the Chicago Cubs in 1969, thus becoming the first second-generation black player in the history of the major leagues. A second son, Sam, Jr., caught in the White Sox organization; and still another son, Jerry Hairston, is currently on the White Sox roster as an outfielder.

*Who are the only three players in major-league history to play 1000 or more games at two different positions (counting the outfield as one position)?*

Only three men—Stan Musial, Ernie Banks and Ron Fairly—have ever played 1000 or more games at two different positions. Musial played 1896 games in the outfield and 1016 at first base; Banks, called "The Greatest Cub Ever," played 1125 games at shortstop and 1259 at first; and Ron Fairly played 1037 games in the outfield and 1218 games at first.

## 8TH INNING

# THE MANAGERS

*Who was the youngest manager in the history of major-league baseball?*

In 1914 Roger Peckinpaugh was appointed manager of the New York Highlanders on the advice of the departing manager, Frank Chance. "Peck" was then the team's starting shortstop and at the ripe old age of 23 added the position of manager to his duties, making him the youngest manager in the history of major-league baseball.

Peckinpaugh went back to playing shortstop the following year (the managerial reins were turned over to "Wild" Bill Donovan) and played shortstop for the next 13 years, being named Most Valuable Player in 1925, the same year he made a record-setting eight errors in the World Series. He next became a manager when he was appointed to the helm of his hometown team, the Cleveland Indians, in 1928, managing them for six years before being replaced by former teammate Walter Johnson in 1933.

Peck was called back into service by the Indians after the famous "Cry Babies Revolt" of 1940 undermined both Cleveland's chances to win the pennant and manager Ossie Vitt's position with the team. Peckinpaugh managed the Indians for only one year on his second tour of duty and then was replaced by *his* shortstop, Lou Boudreau. Boudreau was just a youthful 24 when he took over the Indians from the man who had been the youngest manager in major-league history, making Boudreau in turn, the second youngest manager in the history of baseball.

*Who was the only man to manage a major-league baseball club and also coach a National Football League team—and play in neither?*

Hugo Bezdek, the coach of Rose Bowl champion University of Oregon—which had just defeated Penn 14—

0 in the 1917 Bowl game—was selected by Pittsburgh Pirates owner Barney Dreyfus to replace Honus Wagner as manager of the Pirates in 1917, in an attempt to restore some of the old glories that once were Pittsburgh's to the last-place team. But Bezdek, one of those many talented athletes around the Pittsburgh area, had never played major-league ball and had no better luck with the Pirates than his predecessor—winding up eighth.

Bezdek returned to the Rose Bowl to coach the wartime Mare Island team to another Rose Bowl victory, then returned to the Pirates. This time with Bezdek at the helm, the Pirates came in fourth for the next two years.

By 1937, after a stint as coach at Penn State, Bezdek was back on the major-league scene, as coach of the expansion Cleveland Rams in the National Football League. But in two years Bezdek's thankless task as head coach of the Rams netted only two victories in 15 games and he resigned, leaving the scene as the only man to manage both a big-league baseball team and a professional football team and never to have played in either.

*Who was the oldest manager in major-league history—when first named?*

The Geritol Award for the oldest manager when first named goes to Tom Sheehan, who at age 66 was named to the position of interim manager by the San Francisco Giants after they fired Bill Rigney in 1960. After finishing fifth, Sheehan was reappointed to his position in the front office the next year, to be succeeded by Al Dark, who brought the Giants up to third place, one year away from their pennant-winning year of 1962.

The oldest manager of all time was, of course, Connie Mack, who managed the Philadelphia A's for 51 years, until the age of 88.

*Name the only trainer who ever became a major-league manager.*

Dusty Cooke, former major-league outfielder and the Philadelphia Phillies' trainer, was named the Phillies' interim manager for 11 games in 1948 to replace the embattled Ben Chapman. Cooke compiled a 6-5 record, only one of a select few Phillies managers who ever had a winning record. He was replaced by Eddie Sawyer, who brought the Phillies to third place the following year and the National League pennant in 1950. But even Sawyer couldn't do what Cooke had done, and when he was discharged in 1960 his won-lost record was below .500, as were most Phillies pilots—except for Cooke, the only trainer who ever became a big-league manager.

*Name the six players who played in the 1951 Giants-Dodgers play-off who went on to become major-league managers.*

No less than six of those players who took part in the 1951 play-off between the Giants and the Dodgers later became major-league managers, five Giants and one Dodger. The five Giants were first baseman Carroll "Whitey" Lockman, later to manage the Cubs; catcher Wes Westrum, who later managed the Mets; second baseman Eddie Stanky, who became the manager of the Cards and the White Sox; shortstop Alvin Dark, who later managed the San Francisco Giants, the Kansas City A's, the Cleveland Indians and the Oakland A's; and utility infielder Bill Rigney, who went on to manage the New York and San Francisco Giants, the Los Angeles and California Angels and the Minnesota Twins. The lone Dodger to later manage was Gil

Hodges, who managed the Washington Senators and the New York Mets. The Dodgers also had a seventh future manager on their squad, Dick Williams, who had played 23 games during the season as a utility infielder. But Williams saw no action in the three-game play-off.

*Who was the only manager to win pennants and World Series in his first two years as a major-league manager?*

Several managers have won pennants in their first year, and a few have won the pennant and the World Series in their first year at the helm of their new teams, but only Ralph Houk won the pennant and the World Series in his first two years as manager with the New York Yankees in 1961 and 1962. Houk, in fact, won pennants in his first *three* years as manager, something only Hughie Jennings of the Tigers had done back in 1907, '08 and '09. But whereas Jennings lost all three World Series, Houk's Yankees beat the Reds and the Giants in 1961 and 1962 and lost to the Dodgers in 1963.

*Who was the first manager of the Milwaukee Brewers?*

The Milwaukee Brewers were one of the original teams in the American League in 1901, an outgrowth of the old Western Association and American League President Ban Johnson's fertile mind. Managed by playing manager Hugh Duffy, they could do no better than eighth place in an eight-team league, finishing seven games behind seventh-place Cleveland. Moved to St. Louis the next year, the same team under new manager Jimmy McAleer finished second to the Chicago White Sox.

Duffy, whose .438 batting average in 1894 is the highest in baseball history, was to recover from his first managing experience and go on to manage three other teams, Philadelphia in the National League and Chicago and Boston in the American. But when he retired in 1922 after eight years of managing, his Boston Red Sox team was no higher than his Milwaukee team had been. And Milwaukee, which had had its franchise shifted to St. Louis, would have to wait until the one-year-old Seattle franchise was moved to the Wisconsin city in 1970 for American League ball to return, this time with Dave Bristol managing.

*What famous manager retired the day that four home runs were hit?*

John McGraw retired as manager of the New York Giants on June 3, 1932, after guiding the Giants to ten pennants and three world championships, on the same day that Lou Gehrig hit four home runs in Philadelphia's Shibe Park.

*What manager won the most games in the major leagues without ever winning a pennant?*

Jimmy Dykes, who won 1407 games in his 21 years as a major-league manager for the Chicago White Sox, Philadelphia A's, Baltimore Orioles, Cincinnati Reds, Detroit Tigers and Cleveland Indians, won the most games as a manager without ever winning a pennant. Dykes's teams only finished over .500 in eight of those 21 years and never finished higher than third, and yet he has just six less career wins as a manager than Miller Huggins had.

*Who was the last playing manager before Frank Robinson?*

The last playing manager before Frank Robinson was appointed player-manager of the 1975 Cleveland Indians was Hank Bauer, who took over in midseason 1961 as manager of the Kansas City A's while still a player. Bauer played six more games before deciding to hang up his spikes on July 21, 1961, and devote his energies to managing exclusively. Before Bauer, Solly Hemus was the playing manager of the St. Louis Cardinals for 24 games in 1959. The last full-time playing manager was Lou Boudreau, who played 81 games for the Indians, leading the tribe to fourth place.

> *Who was the first college coach to manage in the majors?*

When his career as a catcher was over in 1907, 26-year-old Wesley Branch Rickey decided to get back to law school and enrolled at the University of Michigan. To supplement his income, he took on the chore of coaching the Michigan baseball team. There he found a tall, strapping, left-handed pitcher named George Sisler, and together they made their way back to the majors with the St. Louis Browns, Sisler as a first baseman and Rickey as a manager. Rickey was thus the first college coach to become a major-league manager, 15 years before Jack Slattery was to make the jump from the Boston College Campus to the Braves.

> *Who was the only man to manage two last-place clubs in one year?*

John McGraw, one of baseball's greatest managers, made history, of a sort, by managing two last-place clubs in one year. In 1902 McGraw jumped in midseason from the fledgling American League to the

National League, leaving the Baltimore Orioles in seventh place and taking many of the Orioles' stars with him to New York, where he took over the reins of the New York Giants. But even though he brought pitcher Joe McGinnity, catcher Roger Bresnahan, first baseman Dan McGann and shortstop–second baseman Billy Gilbert to the Giants, they finished seven and a half games out of seventh. The Orioles, left to the temporary kind care of McGraw's old teammate and current business partner, Wilbert Robinson, and minus some of their star players, floundered and ultimately also finished in eighth place, three and a half games out of seventh in the American League.

The next year found the Orioles and Wilbert Robinson in New York as well, with the Orioles becoming the New York Highlanders and under Clark Griffith finishing in fourth place. Robinson, known as "Uncle Robbie," joined McGraw and his expatriates and made a run for the pennant, finishing in second place behind pennant-winning Pittsburgh.

McGraw went on to win nine pennants and three World Series in his 33 years as a manager, and finished last only one other time——in 1915 when the Giants finished last, just three and a half games out of fourth, with the highest last-place percentage of all time, .454. He retired as the second "winningest" manager of all time on June 3, 1932, with the Giants in the same place they had been when he found them ——last place.

## 9TH INNING

# THE TEAMS

*Which major-league team did not have a single player
with at least 100 hits for an entire season?*

The most impotent clubs are reputed to have been the
1942 Phillies and the 1916 Philadelphia A's, who led their
leagues in most losses, fewest hits, fewest runs scored,
highest ERA, most bases on balls given up by their pitchers,
and totally anemic efforts, finishing 18½ and 40 games out
of seventh place, respectively. But both teams had at least
four players with 100 or more hits on their rosters.

It remained for the 1972 Mets, a team just one year
away from the National League pennant, to produce a team
that hit .225 and produced no batter with at least 100 hits
for the entire year. Beset with injuries to Rusty Staub and
Jerry Grote, the leading producer of hits on the 1972 Mets
was Tommie Agee with but 96.

*Before the Cincinnati Reds won the 1975 and 1976
World Series, name the last National League team to
win back-to-back Series.*

In the 73-year history of the World Series, the American
League has won 44 of the Series played and the National
League only 29. And only three times have National
League teams repeated as World Champions. The first time
was the back-to-back wins of the Chicago Cubs over the
Detroit Tigers in 1907 and 1908, and the last time was
the Cincinnati Reds' back-to-back wins over the Boston
Red Sox and the New York Yankees in 1975 and 1976.
The only other time a National League team repeated was
in 1921 and 1922, when the New York Giants beat the
New York Yankees in two consecutive Series.

*What pennant-winning team finished farthest ahead
of its second-place runner-up?*

The 1902 Pittsburgh Pirates won 103 games and lost just
36 as they completely outclassed their nearest competitors,
finishing 27½ games ahead of second-place Brooklyn.

*What was the only baseball team ever named for a commercial product?*

Many clubs' nicknames have come from someone associated with the club—like the Brooklyn Robins, named after manager Wilbert Robinson; and the Cleveland Naps, named after team captain Napoleon Lajoie—but the only team that took its name directly from a product was the Brooklyn club of the Federal League.

Robert B. Ward owned the Brooklyn club in the new Federal League, created in 1914 to compete on an equal footing with the two established leagues. He also owned Tip Top Bakeries in Brooklyn. The name of the team, known as "The Feds" to most, became the Brooklyn Tip Tops, and it numbered among its ranks for its two years of existence Lee Magee, Benny Kauff ("The Ty Cobb of the Federal League") and Hooks Wiltse. Nonetheless, all it had to show for its effort was some free advertising for its bread and a fifth-and seventh-place finish in the league's two years.

*What team has the most representatives in the Hall of Fame?*

Since the Hall of Fame first opened its portal to the greats of baseball with the induction of Cobb, Ruth, Wagner, Mathewson and Johnson in 1936, no less than 151 men have been inducted into those hallowed halls. However, with very few exceptions, like Johnson or Ted Lyons, an inductee played with more than one team, and therefore doesn't belong to any one team but to several.

But he may have achieved his greatness with one, and on that basis the team with the most representatives in the Hall of Fame is the Boston National League team with 36 men in the Hall of Fame, followed by the New York National League team with 31 and the New York American League team with 29. Among those 36 are Cy Young, who won his 511th game as a member of the Braves; Babe

Ruth, who hit his 714th homer as a member of the Braves; Warren Spahn, who won 356 games as a member of the Braves; Christy Mathewson, who served as president of the Braves; and Maranville, Marquard, Evers, Stengel and Earl Averill, who all ended their careers with the Braves.

> *Name the only club to go from first place one year to last place the next.*

Beaten by the Boston Braves in four straight games in the most surprising upset in all baseball history, the 1914 Philadelphia A's were beset on one side by player defections to the new Federal League and on the other by player holdouts. Manager .Connie Mack, frustrated and embarrassed, saw some of the greatest stars of a team that had won four pennants and three World Series in five years desert his humiliated team.

Mack himself contributed to its fall from power by trading and selling most of the rest of his stars during the winter. Gone was Home Run Baker, who held out the entire 1915 season. Gone were Eddie Plank and Chief Bender, who jumped to the Federal League. And also to go were Eddie Collins, sold to the White Sox for $50,000; Jack Barry, who went to the Red Sox; and all of the other stars of the 1914 team, in a wholesale housecleaning.

The result was the 1915 team, a team that was to win but 43 games, 56 fewer than the previous year, use a record number of 27 pitchers looking for the right formula, and be the only team to go from first place to eighth place in one season.

> *Name the only pennant-bound team to have no-hitters thrown at them on two successive days.*

The 1917 White Sox, on their way to the American League pennant by nine games over their closest pursuers, found themselves on the receiving end of a double dose of no-hit pitching on two successive days early in the season. Meeting the lowly St. Louis Browns, destined to just nose out Philadelphia for seventh place, Chicago was no-hit by Ernest Koob in a single game on May 5 and then, after losing the first game of a doubleheader 8–4 the following day, were the victims of a no-hitter thrown by St. Louis's Bob Groom in the nightcap. This was the last no-hitter thrown by a Browns pitcher until Bobo Holloman's no-hitter 36 years later, to the day, on May 6, 1953.

One other pennant-bound team participated in no-hitters on two successive days, but was the victim in just one of them, as first-place St. Louis and second-place San Francisco swapped no-hitters on September 17 and 18, 1968. On the 17th, Giants pitcher Gaylord Perry pitched a no-hitter against the Cardinals. The following day the Cards' Ray Washburn came right back to no-hit the Giants. And on two momentous days there were two no-hitters thrown in the majors: On May 2, 1917, there was the "double no-hit game" between Toney and Vaughn; and on April 22, 1898, Ted Breitenstein of Cincinnati threw his second no-hitter, this time against Pittsburgh, and Jim Hughes of Baltimore pitched one against Boston.

*What was the last award ever won by a St. Louis Brown?*

Little did anyone realize when Roy Sievers won the American League Rookie of the Year Award in 1949 that it would be the last award ever won by a member of the St. Louis Browns. For 52 seasons the St. Louis Browns had managed a winning percentage of only .433—the worst in major-league history—only five first-division finishes in their last 28 years, one American League pennant in 1944, two home-run champions, one pitching champion and three batting champions—and Roy Sievers, the last Brownie ever to win an award, and the American League's first Rookie of the Year.

*What was the only game in which a team went in—
both as a team and as individuals—with exactly the
same batting average they came out with?*

The pitching sensation of the 1939 season was a 20-year-
old fireballer out of Van Meter, Iowa, nicknamed "Rapid
Robert" Feller. Feller had led the American League in
victories, complete games, innings pitched, strikeouts and
shutouts and now seemed on the verge of real greatness.
His first opponents during the 1940 season were the
Chicago White Sox, whom he was called upon to open the
season against in the Opening Day game at Chicago's
Comiskey Park on April 16. The now-21-year-old Feller,
with three one-hitters already, added to his luster by pitching the first of his three no-hitters against the Sox. He
struck out eight and walked five in setting the White Sox
down without a hit, leaving both the individual batters and
the entire team with the same batting average they had
started the season with just hours before—.000.

Feller's Opening Day no-hitter was neither the first
Opening Day no-hitter nor the earliest no-hitter ever
pitched in a season. Back on April 15, 1909, Leon "Red"
Ames, pitching for the Giants against the Dodgers, had
pitched an Opening Day no-hitter for nine innings. But because the Giants had also failed to score for him, Ames
tried to continue his mastery into extra innings, and lost it
in the 13th after allowing seven extra-inning hits. And
Eddie Cicotte hurled a no-hitter on April 14, 1917, the
second day of the season, two days earlier than Feller's
masterpiece and the earliest no-hitter in a season. But
neither time did the opposing team—both as individual
batters and as a team—go into the game and emerge with
the same batting average.

*What was the alternate name chosen for the Phila-
delphia Phillies in 1944?*

When Robert M. Carpenter bought the Philadelphia Phillies in 1944 for $400,000, the first thing he did was name his son, Robert, as the club president. His next move was to initiate a contest to rename the team. The name chosen for the Phillies was the Bluejays, a name that survived only one year and was never really used by the writers or the Philadelphia fans, who continued to call them Phillies.

Since the New York Highlanders became the New York Yankees in 1913, the only other team to attempt a name change was the Boston Braves, which changed its name to the Boston Bees in 1936. But the name neither took nor helped, and by 1941 they were the Boston Braves again, and still in the second division.

*What team had the only all-switch-hitting infield in baseball history?*

The Los Angeles Dodgers of 1965 and part of 1966 had the only all-switch-hitting infield in baseball history, with Wes Parker playing first, Jim Lefebvre at second, Maury Wills at short and Junior Gilliam at third. The St. Louis Cardinals for a brief period in 1971 had the only catching staff with two switch-hitting catchers on it, when Bob Stinson joined Ted Simmons for 17 games behind the plate.

*What two existing ball parks were used by now-defunct teams in the World Series?*

The Boston Braves, now the Atlanta Braves by way of Milwaukee, played their two home games in the 1914 World Series in Fenway Park, where they beat the heavily favored A's both times to register the first sweep of a World Series, 4–0. And the Milwaukee Braves played their 1957 and 1958 games in the present home of the Milwaukee Brewers, Milwaukee County Stadium, where they won four out of the seven games played against the Yankees in the two Series.

## ABOUT THE AUTHOR

To those who ask the final trivia question—"Who is Bert Randolph Sugar?"—he is the former editor-in-chief of *Argosy* magazine, *Baseball Monthly*, *Boxing Illustrated*, *Gridiron*, *Basketball News*, *Who's Who in Hockey*, and *Dimensions in Living*. A former Quiz Kid, lawyer and advertising agency vice-president and director of marketing, Mr. Sugar lives in "a lovely house overlooking a beautiful mortgage" in Chappaqua, New York, with a bemused and long-suffering wife, two children, four cats and a growing collection of baseball memorabilia.

# FUN & GAMES FOR EVERYONE

| | | | |
|---|---|---|---|
| ____ | 16491 | THE BACKGAMMON QUIZ BOOK | $2.50 |
| | | Prince Joli Kansil | |
| ____ | 16599 | CROSSWORDS WITH THEMES #1 | $1.75 |
| | | Maura Jacobson | |
| ____ | 16640 | CROSSWORDS WITH THEMES #2 | $1.75 |
| | | Maura Jacobson | |
| ____ | 16698 | CROSSWORDS WITH THEMES #3 | $1.75 |
| | | Maura Jacobson | |
| ____ | 16748 | CROSSWORDS WITH THEMES #4 | $1.75 |
| | | Maura Jacobson | |
| ____ | 16760 | FASTER THAN A SPEEDING BULLET | $2.25 |
| | | Stuart Silver & Isidore Haiblum | |
| ____ | 21119 | THE PLAYBOY\WINNER'S GUIDE TO BOARD GAMES | $2.95 |
| ____ | 16710 | PLAYBOY'S PARTY JOKES #1 | $1.95 |
| ____ | 16715 | PLAYBOY'S PARTY JOKES #2 | $1.95 |
| ____ | 16720 | PLAYBOY'S PARTY JOKES #3 | $1.95 |
| ____ | 16725 | PLAYBOY'S PARTY JOKES #4 | $1.95 |
| ____ | 16730 | PLAYBOY'S PARTY JOKES #5 | $1.95 |
| ____ | 16735 | PLAYBOY'S PARTY JOKES #6 | $1.95 |
| ____ | 16893 | WORD FINDS WITH THEMES #1 | $1.95 |
| | | Maura Jacobson | |
| ____ | 16978 | WORD FINDS WITH THEMES #2 | $1.95 |
| | | Maura Jacobson | |
| ____ | 16606 | THE WORLD'S GREATEST HOAXES | $1.95 |
| | | Richard Saunders | |

.1281-3

**PLAYBOY PAPERBACKS**
Book Mailing Service
P.O. Box 690 Rockville Centre, New York 11571

NAME_____

ADDRESS_____

CITY_____STATE_____ZIP_____

Please enclose 50¢ for postage and handling if one book is ordered;
25¢ for each additional book. $1.50 maximum postage and handling
charge. No cash, CODs or stamps. Send check or money order.

Total amount enclosed: $_____